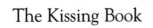

The Kissing Book

Tomima Edmark

EVERYTHING YOU NEED TO KNOW

The Kissing Book

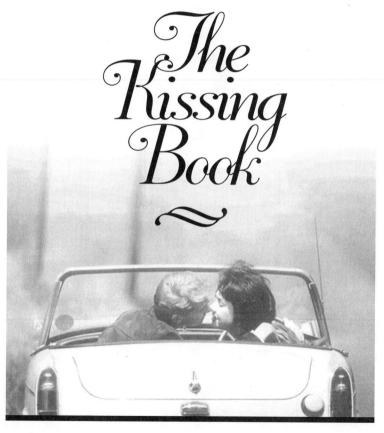

THE SUMMIT PUBLISHING GROUP • ARLINGTON, TEXAS

THE SUMMIT PUBLISHING GROUP
One Arlington Centre, 1112 East Copeland Road, Fifth Floor
Arlington, Texas 76011

Printed in the United States of America.

00 99 98 97 96   010   5 4 3 2 1

Library of Congress Cataloging-in-Publication Data

Edmark, Tomima.
    The kissing book : everything you need to know / by Tomima Edmark.
        p. cm.
    ISBN 1-56530-228-1
    1. Kissing.   I. Title.
GT2640.E355 1996   96-45844
394--dc21   CIP

Cover and book design by David Sims

Table of Contents

Section Three

Kissing as an Art Form

Introduction

A KISS...that beautiful, magical gesture between two people that sends hearts pattering off course, transforms knees into linguine, and propels minds into orbit. Isn't it great? Even the mere mention of kissing brings a smile to one's face (or at least a soft glow) as a special memory comes to mind. Why then has kissing never been fully examined?

The early sixties marked the beginning of what has become a bombardment of books, articles, infomercials, CD-ROMs, and web sites loaded with advice on sexual intercourse. Let's face it: We have become a society which suffers from sex information overload. Yet the romantic kiss, that first act of physical affection for most of us, never has been addressed or properly analyzed.

Most people believe they don't need kissing advice because they instinctively know how to do it right. Well, ask any woman who has walked away from a kiss with facial stubble burn, or any man who has lost his pucker because the woman insisted on kissing and talking at the same time; they'll beg to differ. There are definitely correct and incorrect ways to kiss.

What woman, for example, hasn't sacrificed the basic body function of breathing to a partner who gave little thought to smashing her nose up against his face? (No, that gasp probably wasn't in ecstasy, but for air!) Then there are the slobberers who lick more than they kiss. With dogs, the habit is endearing; with humans, it's loathsome. The power kissers smooch under the delusion that the harder it is the better. And, of course, there are those whose idea of a successful "French kiss" means tackling your uvula with their tongue. I could go on and on, but here's the point: There's much to be learned about this kissing business.

The goal of *The Kissing Book* is to teach you and amuse you, regardless of your current expertise. First-time kissers will find a surefire kissing approach presented here, with step-by-step instructions that should reduce anxiety over that initial romantic kiss. The more experienced kissers will be able to expand their repertoire with an extensive list of kisses and embraces. Kissers in long-standing relationships will find a section on how to take kissing to an extraordinary level and perhaps rekindle an ebbing romantic fire.

The first section, "Prelude to a Kiss," presents a variety of kissing factoids to enlighten you on this enjoyable activity. "Kissing Fundamentals" breaks down all the variables that go into the act of kissing. Think of these chapters as your kissing "how-to" section. Finally, "Kissing as an Art Form" builds on all the previous chapters to present you with a variety of new ways to enhance your kissing style, even if you are already a smooching scholar.

The great thing about kissing is that it is not restricted to only those who are married. It's the inalienable right of every man, woman, and child to kiss. With this in mind, I hope this book establishes two facts: Kissing is one of the most intimate forms of human contact, and it is a very important step in romance. No longer should kissing be regarded merely as a warm-up to whoopee. Kissing can stand on its own and should be given the time and attention it deserves.

Prelude to a Kiss

What a Kiss Is

A Kiss is Just a Kiss—But What's a Kiss?

HAT IS A KISS? This simple and straight-forward question has no easy answer. The *Webster's New Collegiate Dictionary* defines the verb "to kiss" as "to touch with the lips." This definition captures the basic action of a kiss, perhaps, but it certainly falls short of a comprehensive explanation. Really, wouldn't you be disappointed to learn that the romantic kiss you just experienced was merely lip grazing? A kiss has emotion, meaning, and expression. But what is a kiss?

Most may feel it is unnecessary to define kissing because we all know what it is. After all, children experience kissing the moment they arrive in this world, when they are instantly showered with them. Kissing then follows us all our lives. However, if we are to fully understand kissing we must be able to explain what it is.

Many have attempted to define the kiss. Some people have taken a rather pragmatic approach:

"The anatomical juxtaposition of two orbicularis oris muscles in a state of contraction."

DR. HENRY GIBBONS, DEFINITION OF A KISS

♥

3

"A kiss is produced by a kind of sucking movement of the muscles of the lips, accompanied by a weaker or louder sound. It must be in contact with a creature or object, otherwise you could be calling a horse."

CHRISTOPHER NYROP

♥

"A pressure of the mouth against the body."
Dictionary of the
DANISH PHILOLOGICAL SOCIETY

♥

"A bite and a suction."

P. D'ENJOY

♥

"An interchange of labial microbes."

SANTIAGE Y CAJALC

♥

"A vigorous exchange of saliva."

ANONYMOUS

♥

Others have been struck by a kiss's sentiment. For example the poet Samuel Coleridge called a kiss "nectar breathing." The old Roman poet, Martial, described a kiss as "the fragrance of balsam extracted from aromatic trees." And Shakespeare defined the kiss as a "seal of love." Others, too, have chosen the passionate and poetic angle:

"A word invented by the poets to rhyme with 'bliss'."

AMBROSE BIERCE

♥

4

"What is a kiss? Why this, as some approve;
The sure sweet cement, glue and lime of love."

ROBERT HERRICK

A *Kiss*, Hesperides

♥

"To a young girl, faith; to a married woman, hope;
to an old maid, charity."

V.P. SKIPPER

♥

"The blossom of love."

ANCIENT GREEK POET

♥

"Kisses are like grains of gold or silver found upon the
ground; of no value themselves, but precious as showing
that a mine is near."

GEORGE VILLIERS

♥

"Love's lesser lightning."

SIR JOHN SUCKLING

♥

I am just two and two, I am warm, I am cold,
And the parents of numbers that cannot be told,
I am lawful, unlawful—a duty, a fault—
I am often sold dear, good for nothing when bought;
An extraordinary boon, and a matter of course,
And yielded with pleasure when taken by force.

WILLIAM COWPER

♥

"Four sweet lips, two pure souls, and one undying affection—these are love's pretty ingredients for a kiss."

CHRISTIAN NESTELL BOVEE

♥

Of course humor can be found in any circumstance. Kissing is no exception. Several witty observations are duly noted:

"A kiss sounds the same as when a cow drags her hind hoof out of a swamp."

OLD GERMAN SAYING

♥

"Lip service to love."

WARREN GOLDBERG

♥

"A pleasant reminder that two heads are better than one."

REX PRAUTY

♥

"Something that often leads to marriage because it leaves something to be desired."

DEFINITION ADAPTED FROM ROBERT FONTAINE

♥

"At twenty a kiss is an experiment, at forty a sentiment, and after that a compliment."

ANONYMOUS

♥

"A thing of use to no one, but prized to two."

ROBERT ZWICKEY

♥

"The kiss is a wordless articulation of desire whose object lies in the future and somewhat to the south."

LANCE MORROW

♥

"A contraction of the mouth due to an enlargement of the heart."

ANONYMOUS

♥

"A kiss is a lovely trick designed by nature to stop speech when words become superfluous."

INGRID BERGMAN

♥

These interpretations encompass a wide range of kissing revelations from the practical to the passionate. The famous writer Elizabeth Meriwether Gilmer (alias Dorothy Dix) was obviously gastronomically inspired when she commented that "Nobody wants to kiss when they are hungry." This assortment of kissing commentaries proves only that a kiss is not easily defined.

When attempting to define a kiss, the lips and mouth must be mentioned; after all, they are a kiss's tools. A kiss also produces a kind of sucking motion which is generated from the lip muscles followed by a sound of lips smacking at various sound levels. However, it could be argued that these same sounds are used to call a horse or dog. For this reason, there must also be an inclusion of lip contact with a living creature or object.

Even if we can't come up with a definitive explanation, it is clear that the phenomenon of kissing plays a very important role throughout one's life. For a child, kissing symbolizes love and approval. It is a reward for being good and is a warm send-off to a good night's sleep. Mom's kisses have magical powers to make the hurt go away. Kissing can even break spells to awaken Sleeping Beauties and turn frogs into princes. So from the start, kissing is a very pleasurable concept.

In adolescence, kissing becomes more complicated with the transition from innocence to romance. Teens find themselves pressured to perform a first romantic kiss before their sixteenth birthday. No longer can kisses be performed by just anyone. Kissing turns into a very serious matter, and, thus, "kissing anxiety" is discovered. Kisses now express additional emotions: friendship, peace, treachery, respect, victory, luck.

Later in life, the kiss marks the first step to love-play and all its physical aspects. Life becomes a game of kiss-chase, searching for the kiss we all dream of, the *Kiss of Love*. When we find it, we use it to seal our marriage vows. Then kissing comes full circle and once again serves as an accepted greeting by friends and family and is a symbol of love and approval.

Because the kiss is so simple in design and easy to perform, we have found other uses for it in addition to those that mark the milestones through life. We kiss to say hello or good-bye. We kiss for luck or for sympathy. We seal things with a kiss. We celebrate with a kiss. We sometimes kiss the ground others walk on. Politicians kiss babies. Men and boys steal kisses; women and girls usually let them. We avoid kissing and telling. We encourage kissing to make up. We try to avoid the Judas kiss, the kiss of death, and kissing the porcelain god. And eventually, we all kiss the dust.

A kiss is the most intimate form of contact between a man and a woman. The mouth and lips are androgynous, allowing partners to communicate as biological equals, so kissing can be considered common ground between the sexes. Unlike any other sensual act, kissing makes each partner aware of what the other is feeling.

The mucous membranes of the lips are the most easily accessible of the body's erogenous zones and perhaps the most important. In fact, the sector of the brain that deals with messages from the lips is larger than that which handles impulses from the entire torso. The lips hold tremendous potential to please. With this symmetry and proximity, it's not difficult to detect what your partner enjoys. Chances are your partner is kissing you the way he or she wishes to be kissed.

Finally, let it be known what kissing is not. It is not flirting; however, flirting can lead to kissing. Kissing is not merely "foreplay" to a greater intimacy. Kissing is capable of starting and ending on its own. It should, therefore, be considered as before foreplay, or "beforeplay," in the orchestration of romance. And kissing is definitely not meaningless. It is filled with significance and emotion.

The Origin of Kissing

THINK ABOUT KISSING for a minute. It's really a rather bizarre act. You pucker the lips that frame your mouth—a damp, germ-infested opening through which food (and who knows what else) passes—and touch another with them. Sort of sounds the same way that eating fried chicken embryos for breakfast does, doesn't it? So where did this kissing idea originate? Why isn't it a rubbing of bellies or a fondling of fingers? And, how was another cajoled into participating?

Surprisingly, there is very little information on kissing to answer these questions. One famous adventurer claimed the kiss to be "as old as creation and yet as young and fresh as ever. It preexisted, still exists, and always will exist." Despite the absence of hard, factual information, there are several theories floating around that try to explain the origin of the kiss. Some hold water; others leak like a sieve.

One theory is based on the fact that early humans discovered the cooling-down effect that salt consumption played on hot days. After looking around, they must have noticed that the skin of their partner presented a very handy source to lick salt from. One thing led to another, and this licking somehow evolved into current-day kissing. While this idea is creative, the notion that kissing evolved from an effort to cool down is hard to concede. Has kissing ever cooled you down?

Kissing may have its roots in early religious rituals. Some authorities claim the existence of an early religious belief that the air man exhaled had magic power and contained one's soul. During their religious ceremonies, participants used a form of the mouth kiss to exchange breath. The inference here is that onlookers must have concluded that it looked like fun and ran off in search of other willing souls.

The kiss could also be a refinement of nose rubbing, which evolved from animal sniffing. Sociologists have noted that the literal translation of "kiss me" in the language of certain tribes is "smell me." It is also well known that Eskimos, Laplanders, and Polynesians greet one another by pressing their noses together and inhaling. So it is possible that the kiss's lineage is rooted in the instinctive sniffing of animals. Now, if you stop for a minute and think where you last observed animals instinctively sniffing each other, you might additionally be glad that humans, like the kiss, have evolved.

There are some who allege the kiss actually developed from the act of biting. Certain animals habitually bite one another during foreplay and the fulfillment of the sex act. Some anthropologists speculate that early humans (in their anthropoid stage of evolution) may have found it necessary to fasten on to their mates during coitus by using their teeth. Even today, many societies, ranging from the lowly to the most highly civilized, use the "love bite" when sexually aroused or during sexual activity. A one word response to this theory is…Ouch!

From biting, we go to the theory of chewing. Before there was baby food, as we know it today, early moms chewed food in their mouth and then fed it to their babies by way of a "kiss." Maybe this is where the phrase "hungry for a kiss" originated?

A more recent theory poses kissing as nothing more than an instinctive action. Some scientists postulate that kissing really is a matter of personal chemistry. All of us have sebaceous skin glands inside our mouths and at the edges of our lips which produce a substance called sebum. Sebum is thought to have a kind of biological signal that when transferred by touch, or kiss, causes a heightened desire for the other person. It follows that "love" may be nothing more than an addiction to another's sebum, and kissing is the vehicle through which you find your sebum of choice.

Now, before you dismiss this theory completely, there is actual research to prove this. Eagles and some other birds bond through an exchange of sebum. During avian mating, the suitor chews a piece of food and then gives it to his mate. In experiments where the suitor's sebaceous glands are removed, the suitee merely pecks at the donor and then flies off with his mating gift. Interesting parallel.

But of all the theories on the origin of kissing, the one that gets the most votes from researchers is as follows: It may be a natural evolution from our birth instinct to suck our mother's breast for nourishment. Or, to put it another way, it is simply a continuation of our desire to be breast-fed. So, what this theory says is that kissing is nothing more than satisfying a feeling of hunger. If this is true, most of us would rather have satiated our hunger with Oreos than to have endured some of the kisses we've received.

Humans don't seem to be the only animals on this earth who kiss. Manifestations resembling the kiss also can be found among various lower animals. Snails, for instance, rub antennae. Birds use their beaks for a kind of caress. Dogs lick their masters as a form of affection. So human beings are not the only animals who enjoy this tactile activity.

The existence of many theories on the kiss's origin is probably attributable to our many diverse cultures and their unique handling of the kiss. For instance, in a large number of African cultures, there is a maternal kiss between mother and child, but no romantic kiss among adults. Before the introduction of Western customs, the Chinese felt the kiss was indecent, both in public and behind closed doors. And the Japanese, though exposed to the kiss, chose to do without it until fairly recently when they adopted many Western

Kissing Games

Post Office

All the girls are out of the room. An area is designated as the post office, and one boy is inside. He selects a girl and tells another boy to tell her she has mail. She goes to the post office and is kissed by the boy inside. She leaves, and the next girl is told to go in and collect her mail from a new postman.

13

traditions. As these examples show, the romantic kiss is not an outgrowth of a more advanced culture or civilization.

Take your pick as to which theory you wish to embrace. Better yet, create one of your own. The truth of the matter is that any attempt at resolution is merely speculation. Very little documentation exists to make one stand out as a better theory than another. Perhaps these words sum it up best:

"There is no author of the first kiss.
Kissing, like many other good things, is anonymous."

ANONYMOUS

♥

Kissing Through the Ages

O HOW LONG has kissing been around, and how has it fared through history? There is very little historical information available to build a complete accounting. However, we do have some facts and findings to help explain how this romantic act of kissing evolved to the form we know today.

Historians are in agreement that the act of kissing as an expression of love is a fairly recent phenomenon. They base this opinion on the fact that Greek poetry scarcely mentions it, and there is no word for it in the Celtic languages. The first known visual representation of a deep romantic kiss was found on Mochica pottery in Peru and dates back to around 200 B.C.

Credit for developing the kiss into a romantic gesture is given to the country of India. Shortly after the Aryan penetration (approximately 1500 B.C.) the Kamasutra was created. The Sanskrit word *Kamasutra* means "love manual." It was a treatise which set forth rules for sensuous and sensual pleasure, love, and marriage according to Hindu law. Included in the Kamasutra were instructions on performing various kisses and when to use them romantically. Its steaminess has stood the test of time. Even today, reading the Kamasutra can make one blush.

Kissing in ancient Egypt was almost unknown. Cleopatra, the great lover, is believed not to have romantically kissed any of her numerous conquests, including Caesar or Mark Antony. Ancient Rome, on the other hand, used kissing as a social gesture to greet friends and family, shopkeepers, salespeople, and basically the rest of the general population.

We know that romantic kissing occurred during the Roman Empire because the nuptial kiss at the altar began during this period. It was said to symbolize the spiritual union between bride and groom as they exchanged "the breath of life." There were also several Roman laws at this time that addressed kissing. One Roman

Kissing Games

Spin the Bottle

Everyone sits in a circle around a bottle placed on its side. One person spins the bottle. The open end is the pointer. If it points to a person of the opposite sex, the spinner and this person kiss in front of the group. Variation: The game is played in a dark room with a flashlight.

law discusses a kiss called the *osculum interveniens*. This was a kiss exchanged between engaged couples. In the event that one of the contracting parties died before the marriage took place, only a portion of the wedding gifts needed to be returned provided a kiss between the couple was exchanged at the engagement. If no *osculum interveniens* was exchanged, all the gifts were to be returned. You would think engaged couples couldn't comply with this law fast enough. Well, the law had a hitch; such a kiss gave the man legal rights to the woman (including sanctions if the marriage plans were canceled) as soon as he bestowed such a betrothal kiss. Talk about a powerful kiss!

Another clue we have to support romantic kissing during the Roman Empire was the existence of three words for kissing. Each word communicated a different kind of kiss. The words they used were:

- **Oscula**—friendly kisses
- **Basia**—kisses of love
- **Suavia**—passionate kisses

During medieval times in Europe, kissing was used with great discretion, both for social and romantic purposes. A kissing hierarchy for social kissing was established during that period. The social ranking of the two individuals determined where the kiss would be placed. The lower you were from them on the status pole, the farther away from their face you kissed. You'd kiss peers on the mouth or cheek, those a notch above you on the hand, those higher still on the knee, and finally those whom you might as well place on a pedestal (primarily religious figures), you kissed on the foot or the ground in front of their feet. This is where the phrase "I kiss the ground you walk on" originates.

Also during this time, a kiss called "the Christian kiss" became an ordained ritual of the Church. Romans 16:16 states "Greet one another with a holy kiss," and people took it literally. Women began to freely kiss their male friends, then claim it to be in the name of the Church. Obviously this type of kissing was getting out of hand, and shortly thereafter laws were put in place to govern such behavior. One French law declared that a woman was guilty of adultery if she kissed or allowed herself to be kissed by any man other than her husband. An Italian law also took kissing very seriously. If a man kissed a girl in public, he could become obligated to marry her.

The Church also came up with the "kiss of peace" during this time. Priests would kiss the penitent, thus giving them peace. This practice later spread beyond the walls of the Church and was used by others to seal the reconciliation of enemies. This kiss, however, disappeared after the Middle Ages.

It was common during those times for men to kiss one another. For example, English knights would kiss each other before a jousting tournament.

Kissing another man as a greeting was actually a sign of trust. Allowing another man such close access to your person proved you trusted him enough to not bite off your ear or stab you in the back. Also, the kiss was used to seal legal contracts between men. Those who could not sign their name would draw an "X" on the signature line and then kiss it. This would then make the contract binding.

The Renaissance (the fourteenth through sixteenth centuries) marked a calmer time due to the revival of education and the questioning of the Church. While other forms of kissing lost popularity, the kiss of greeting or friendship remained. In England, hosts would welcome their guests by encouraging them to kiss each family member on the lips. Fashion dictated that everyone should give and receive kisses, but many considered this a real nuisance. People began to file suits for being wrongfully kissed. Peasants or lowly citizens were forbidden to kiss nobles, so punishment was more severe for such a kiss than the mere kissing between the same social class.

In 1665, London's Great Plague (which lasted almost a year and killed 68,596) put a damper on the popular act of social kissing. The fear of catching something from a neighbor made tipping hats, bowing, curtsying, and waving hands the new popular greeting gestures.

France, during this time, continued with the popular act of social kissing. King Louis XIII of France (1610–1643) was famous for kissing every woman in Normandy. He used the sham of granting his Royal Benediction.

The late eighteenth century marked the beginning of the Industrial Revolution, particularly in England. People began migrating from the countryside to the big cities in search of work. With so many strangers, the friendly lip kiss greetings no longer felt comfortable. Hand kissing became the new standard greeting, which over time evolved into the hand-shake greeting we are all familiar with today.

A German jurist wrote a treatise at this time classifying kisses as either lawful or unlawful. Lawful kisses were spiritu-al, reconciliatory, customary, respectful, or loving gestures between married or engaged persons, family, or friends. Treacherous, malicious, or lustful kisses were considered unlawful. Thus, women could bring suit against men who kissed them against their will.

Kafkaesque kiss
A kiss that starts out feeling like it's about to transform you but ends up just bugging you.

In 1837, an Englishman by the name of Thomas Saverland brought suit against Caroline Newton for brutally biting his nose after he playfully tried to kiss her. The judge acquitted Miss Newton, stating "When a man kisses a woman against her will, she is fully entitled to bite his nose if she so pleases."

The term "French kiss" came into the English language in 1923. It was actually considered a slang term or a slur on the French culture, which was thought to be overly con-cerned with sexual matters. The truth of the matter is the French call such a kiss a "tongue kiss" or "soul kiss."

Throughout history, some general observations can be made about kissing. For one, social kissing has been used more by the upper crust or elite than any other social group. The mouth most desirable for kissing has always been described as well formed, red as coral or roses, sweet, and soft.

Today, the use of kissing is widespread. Where the public display of affection (P.D.A) was highly frowned upon in etiquette books at the beginning of the twentieth century, today it is a very common practice. Our current casual attitude toward public kissing is probably attributed to our increased exposure to the many other cultures which feature kissing openly in public.

Kissing Quotes

ANY HAVE SHARED their thoughts on the subject of kissing. This chapter captures their varied reflections, from the heartfelt to the hilarious. One thing is for sure, you will enjoy browsing this chapter.

Kissing According to the Famous

"The kiss originated when the first male reptile licked the first female reptile, implying in a subtle, complimentary way that she was as succulent as the small reptile he had for dinner the night before."

F. SCOTT FITZGERALD

♥

"Hollywood's the place where they'll pay you a thousand
dollars for a kiss and fifty cents for your soul."

MARILYN MONROE

♥

"Few men know how to kiss well; fortunately, I've always
had time to teach them."

MAE WEST

♥

"I get no respect from my wife. She kisses the dog, but she
won't drink out of my glass."

RODNEY DANGERFIELD

♥

"What is a kiss? An inquiry on the second floor as to
whether the first floor is free."

ART GARFUNKEL

♥

"Political baby-kissing must come to an end, unless the size
and the age of the babies be materially increased."

W.C. FIELDS

♥

"Everybody winds up kissing
the wrong person good night."

ANDY WARHOL

♥

"A kiss on the wrist feels good, but a diamond bracelet
lasts forever."

ADLAI STEVENSON
Address to Chicago Council on Foreign Relations

♥

2 1

"Two people kissing always look like fish."

ANDY WARHOL

♥

"I kissed my first woman and smoked my first cigarette on
the same day. I have never had time for tobacco since."

ARTURO TOSCANINI

♥

"You know Mr. (D. W.) Griffith told us we must never kiss
actors—it isn't healthy."

DOROTHY GISH

♥

"I wasn't kissing her, I was whispering in her mouth."

CHICO MARX
caught kissing a chorus girl by his wife

♥

Ageless Advice

"On every maiden's lips the kiss sits like a rose
which only longs to be plucked."

GOLIARD SAYING

♥

"A kiss once given is never lost."

ITALIAN PROVERB

♥

"A kiss that speaks volumes is seldom a first edition."

ANONYMOUS

♥

"A lisping lass is good to kiss."

OLD PROVERB

♥

"In love, there is always one who kisses and one who offers the cheek."

FRENCH PROVERB

♥

"Before you kiss a handsome prince, you have to kiss a lot of frogs."

TWENTIETH-CENTURY PROVERB

♥

"A kiss without a mustache is like an egg without salt."

OLD SPANISH SAYING

♥

"A man often kisses the hand he would rather cut off."

SPANISH, PORTUGUESE, DANISH, TURKISH, AND SWAHILI PROVERB

♥

"He kissed her so that it rang just as it does when one strikes the horns off felled cows."

DANISH EXPRESSION

♥

Here's to the smoke that curls in the air
Here's to the dog at my feet;
Here's to the girls that have gone before,
Gad! but their kisses were sweet!

OLD DRINKING TOAST

♥

Here's to the girl with eyes of brown,
If you ask for a kiss she will call you down;
Here's to the girl with eyes of blue,
If you ask for one—she will say, yes, take two.

OLD DRINKING TOAST

♥

Kissing Witticisms

Oh, innocent victims of Cupid,
Remember this terse little verse;
To let a fool kiss you is stupid,
To let a kiss fool you is worse."

E. Y. HARBURG

♥

"The honeymoon is over when the kiss that was a
temptation becomes an obligation."

ANONYMOUS

♥

"To kiss or not to kiss is one of the most important
questions of the twentieth century, a question which is
normally answered *No!* and acted *Yes!*"

DR. ALBERT ELLIS

♥

"Kissing is the most pleasant way of
spreading germs yet devised."

ANONYMOUS

♥

"Lord, I wonder what fool it was that first invented kissing!"

JONATHAN SWIFT

"Polite Conversation"

♥

"Lots of things have been started by kisses,
especially young things."

ANONYMOUS

♥

"In fifty years kissing will be unheard of—
but in fifty years, who cares?"

A PHYSICIAN WISHING TO REMAIN ANONYMOUS

♥

"Stealing a kiss may be petty larceny,
but sometimes it's grand."

ANONYMOUS

♥

"Be plain in dress, and sober in your diet:
In short, my deary, kiss me and be quiet."

LADY MARY WORTLEY MONTAGUE

♥

"It's a good idea to kiss the children good night,
if you don't mind waiting up for them."

ANONYMOUS

♥

"Traditional Hollywood-style greeting
for friend and foe alike."

EUGENE E. BRUSSELL

♥

"There are certain tasks where you want personal interaction rather than dealing directly with a computer, like necking."

ANONYMOUS

♥

"Kissing is where two people get so close together they can't see anything wrong with each other."

A PSYCHOLOGIST WISHING TO REMAIN ANONYMOUS

♥

"A kiss is not enough for one, just enough for two, and too much for three."

ANONYMOUS

♥

Kisses from the Heart

The sunlight clasps the earth
And the moonbeams kiss the sea:
What are all these kissings worth
If thou kiss not me.

PERCY BYSSHE SHELLEY

♥

You must remember this, a kiss is still a kiss,
A sigh is just a sigh;
The fundamental things apply,
As time goes by."

HERMAN HUPFELD

"Everybody's Welcome." Also in the film Casablanca

♥

Honeyed seal of soft affections,
Tenderest pledge of future bliss,
Dearest tie of young connections,
Love's first snowdrop, virgin kiss.

ROBERT BURNS

♥

I gently raised her sweet, pure face,
Her eyes with radiant, love sight filled.
That trembling kiss I'll ne'er forget
Which both our hearts with rapture filled.

EXCERPT FROM POEM "THREE KISSES"

♥

A kiss, when all is said…,tis a secret
Told to the mouth instead of the ear.

CYRANO DE BERGERAC

♥

"Four sweet lips, two pure souls, and one undying
affection—these are love's pretty ingredients for a kiss."

CHRISTIAN NESTELL BOVEE

♥

"It is the passion that is in a kiss that gives to its sweetness;
it is the affection in a kiss that sanctifies it."

CHRISTIAN NESTELL BOVEE

♥

"Graze on my lips, and if those hills be dry, stray lower,
where the pleasant fountains lie."

WILLIAM SHAKESPEARE
Venus and Adonis

♥

27

"A soft lip would tempt you to eternity of kissing!"
BEN JONSON
♥

"A kiss is a rosy dot over the 'I' of loving."
CYRANO DE BERGERAC
♥

"The splash of the waves
against the pebbles of the beach
is like the sound of long kisses."
JOHANNES JORGENSEN
♥

"The kiss you take is paid by that you give:
The joy is mutual, and I'm still in debt."
LORD LANSDOWNE
♥

"Hang up love's mistletoe over the earth,
and let us kiss under it all the year round."
ANONYMOUS
♥

"Once he drew, with one long kiss,
my whole soul through my lips."
ALFRED, LORD TENNYSON
♥

"For love or lust, for good or ill,
behold the kiss is potent still."
JOHN RICHARD MORELAND
The Kiss
♥

"Is not a kiss the very autograph of love?"

HENRY T. FINCK

♥

"The sound of a kiss is not so loud as that of a cannon,
but its echo lasts a great deal longer."

OLIVER WENDELL HOLMES

The Professor at the Breakfast Table, Chapter 11

♥

"I understand thy kisses, and thou mine,
And that's a feeling disputation."

WILLIAM SHAKESPEARE

Henry IV, Part One

♥

Give me a kisse and to that kisse a score;
Then to that twenty, add a hundred more:
And thousand to that hundred: so kisse on,
To make that thousand up a million;
Treble that million, and when that is done,
Let's kisse afresh, as when we first begun.

ROBERT HERRICK

To Anthea: Oh, My Anthea, Hesperides

♥

"Kisses kept are wasted,
love is to be tasted."

EDMOND VANCE COOKE

Kisses Kept are Wasted

♥

A Female Perspective

....

Tho' a kiss be amiss
She who misses the kisses,
As Miss without kiss,
May miss being Mrs.

JULIA LOCKHEART
The Eternals
♥

"Kissing him would be like kissing barbed wire."

ROSEMARIE JARSKI
♥

"To a woman the first kiss is the end of the beginning;
to a man it is the beginning of the end."

HELEN ROWLAND
Reflections of a Bachelor Girl
♥

"Marriage is the miracle that transforms a kiss
from a pleasure into a duty."

HELEN ROWLAND
♥

"Every time some men plant a kiss
they expect to reap a harvest."

ANONYMOUS
♥

"When a man tells you your kisses are intoxicating,
watch out. He is probably mixing his drinks."

ANONYMOUS
♥

"A man snatches the first kiss, pleads for the second,
demands the third, takes the fourth, accepts the fifth
—and endures all the rest."

HELEN ROWLAND

♥

"My child, if you finally decide to let a man kiss you,
put your whole heart and soul into it.
No man likes to kiss a rock."

LADY CHESTERFIELD

♥

"A kiss can be a comma, a question mark,
or an exclamation point.
That's basic spelling that every woman ought to know."

MISTINGUETTE
French dancer

♥

A Masculine Perspective

"It was like putting your mouth against an automatic bank
teller, where it swallows your credit card."

JOHN UPDIKE

♥

"Don't wait to know her better to kiss her; kiss her,
and you'll know her better."

ANONYMOUS

♥

"Kissing her lips was like kissing warm but uncooked liver."

STEPHEN KING

♥

"Any man who can drive safely while kissing a pretty girl is simply not giving the kiss the attention it deserves."

ANONYMOUS

"It's impossible to kiss a girl unexpectedly only sooner than she thought you would."

ANONYMOUS

"You may conquer with the sword, but you are conquered by a kiss."

DANIEL HEINSIUS

"Kissing a girl is like opening a jar of olives—hard to get the first one, but the rest come easy."

ANONYMOUS

"I am in favor of preserving the French habit of kissing ladies' hands—after all, one must start somewhere."

SACHA GUITRY

"The trouble with girls who are highbrows is that they would rather be osculated than kissed."

ANONYMOUS

"If you are ever in doubt as to whether or not you should kiss a pretty girl, always give her the benefit of the doubt."

THOMAS CARLYLE

"A man who kisses every girl he meets gets a lot of
rebuffs—also a lot of kisses."

ANONYMOUS

♥

"Kissing and bussing differ in this:
We buss our Wantons, but our Wives we kiss."

ROBERT HERRICK

♥

"If your wife kisses you when you get home,
is it affection or inspection?"

ANONYMOUS

♥

"Alas, that women do not know,
kisses make men loath to go."

ROBERT JONES

♥

"Some girls blush when they are kissed, and some swear;
but the worst are those who laugh."

ANONYMOUS

♥

"A boy becomes a man when he decides it's more fun to
steal a kiss than second base."

ANONYMOUS

♥

"When women kiss, it always reminds me of
prizefighters shaking hands."

H. L. MENCKEN

♥

"He who has stolen a kiss and knows not how to steal the
rest deserves to forfeit his advantage."

OVID

Art of Love

♥

"The difference between a man kissing his sister
and a pretty girl is about fifty-five seconds."

ANONYMOUS

♥

"Kissing don't last; cookery do!"

GEORGE MEREDITH

♥

Sentimental Definitions

"That you cannot give without taking
and cannot take without giving."

ANONYMOUS

♥

"A kiss is one of the most potent stimulants
that a man or woman can indulge in."

SHEIKH NEFZAWI

♥

"It is a noun both common and proper,
not very singular; and agrees with both you and me."

ANONYMOUS

♥

"Soul meets soul on lover's lips."

PERCY BYSSHE SHELLEY

♥

"A kiss is the twenty-seventh letter of the alphabet
the love-labial which it takes two to speak plainly."
OLIVER WENDELL HOLMES
♥

Lip Service

A peach is a peach,
A plum is a plum,
A kiss ain't a kiss, without some tongue.
So open your mouth,
and close your eyes,
and give your tongue… some exercise!
ANONYMOUS
♥

"If you kiss enough asses, you'll get kicked in the teeth."
GERALD BARZAN
♥

"Give me another naughty, naughty kiss before we part."
PLAUTUS
Asinaria, Act V, sc. 2
♥

"Never a lip is curved with pain
that can't be kissed into smile again."
BRET HARTE
The Last Galleon
♥

"Stolen kisses are always sweetest."
LEIGH HUNT
♥

"The greatest sin 'twixt heaven and hell
Is first to kiss and then to tell."

ANONYMOUS

♥

"The lips that have been innocent of passion's kiss
frequently ooze with gossip's poison."

ELLA WHEELER WILCOX

♥

The hole in the face is called the mouth
For getting in and giving out,
For every kiss there is a bite,
The tongue hangs long, the lips lock tight.

ANONYMOUS

♥

"Do not make me kiss, and you will not make me sin."

H.G. BOHN
Hand-Book of Proverbs

♥

"Formerly a kiss used to follow a nice evening, but
nowadays a nice evening follows a kiss."

ANONYMOUS

♥

"Wounds from a friend are better than kisses from an
enemy!"

PROVERBS 27:6

♥

Apple pie without some cheese
Is like a kiss without a squeeze.

PRINTED ON THE NAPKINS OF A DINER

♥

Pretty red lips as soft as a rose.
How many have kissed them,
God only knows.

ANONYMOUS

♥

Let us drink to the thought that wherever a man roves
He is sure to find something blissful and dear,
And that when he is far from the lips that he loves,
He can always make love to the lips that are near.

TOM MOORE

♥

"Benjy. The kiss. There are all sorts of kisses, lad,
from the sticky confection to the kiss of death.
Of them all, the kiss of an actress is the most unnerving.
How can we tell if she means it or if she's just practicing?"

RUTH GORDON

The Leading Lady, Act 2

♥

The purest kiss in the world is this:
The kiss that a mother lays
On her boy's fresh lips
As he blithely trips
To meet the world and its ways.

ANONYMOUS

♥

"We have kissed away kingdoms and provinces."

WILLIAM SHAKESPEARE

Antony and Cleopatra

♥

Take heed that when upon her lips you seize,
You press them not too hard lest it displease.

OVID

Art of Love

♥

"To love platonically and to kiss is as absurd
as a hunger-striker who would carry out his purpose
by becoming a vegetarian."

BAUER

♥

"Kissing a smoker is like licking a dirty ashtray."

ANONYMOUS

♥

Kissing in the Movies

Groucho: "Where is your husband?"
Dumont: "Why, he's dead."
Groucho: "I'll bet he's just using that as an excuse."
Dumont: "I was with him to the very end."
Groucho: "No wonder he passed away."
Dumont: "I held him in my arms and kissed him."
Groucho: "Oh, I see. Then it was murder."
    —Dialogue from the movie *Duck Soup* (Paramount, 1933)

♥

"A girl should never kiss a man she doesn't intend to marry."
    —Judy Garland in *Little Nellie Kelly* (MGM, 1940)

♥

"Where do the noses go?"
    —Ingrid Bergman to Gary Cooper, *For Whom The Bell Tolls* (Paramount, 1943)

"Hey, hey mister! Come back out here! I'll show you a kiss that'll put hair back on your head!"
    —James Stewart, *It's A Wonderful Life* (RKO, 1946)

"I love him because he doesn't know how to kiss—the jerk."
    —Barbara Stanwyck about Gary Cooper, *Ball of Fire* (Fox, 1941)

"It's even better when you help."
    —A critical Lauren Bacall speaking to an inert Humphrey Bogart in *To Have and Have Not* (Warner Bros., 1944)

"Here's a soldier of the South who loves you, Scarlett, wants to feel your arms around him, wants to carry the memory of your kisses into battle with him. Never mind about loving me. You're a woman sending a soldier to his death with a beautiful memory. Scarlett, kiss me. Kiss me, once."
    —Clark Gable leaving Vivien Leigh for war, *Gone With The Wind* (MGM,1939)

"Cross my heart, and kiss my elbow."
>—Audrey Hepburn, *Breakfast at Tiffany's* (Paramount, 1961)

♥

"Wanna dance or do you just want to suck face?"
>—Henry Fonda, *On Golden Pond* (Universal, 1981)

♥

"There's something terribly uncomplimentary in apologizing for kissing a beautiful woman."
>—Richard Arlen to Ida Lupino, *Artists and Models* (Paramount, 1937)

♥

"From now on, I've got to know the name of every man that kisses me."
>—Ida Lupino, *Artists and Models* (Paramount, 1937)

♥

"Frankly, my child, I had a sudden, powerful, and very ignoble desire to kiss you till your lips were somewhat bruised."
>—David Niven bluntly confessing his desire to Maggie McNamara, *The Moon Is Blue* (United Artists, 1953)

♥

"I will not have my face smeared with lipstick. If you want to kiss me, kiss me on the lips, which is what a merciful providence provided them for."
>—Herbert Marshall speaking to Gene Tierney, *The Razor's Edge* (Fox, 1946)

♥

"I don't know why I should act so experienced. It was only my second kiss this year."
> —Diane Varsi confessing to Russ Tamblyn, *Peyton Place* (Fox, 1957)

♥

"Kissing your hand may make you feel very, very good, but a diamond and sapphire bracelet lasts forever."
> —Marilyn Monroe, *Gentlemen Prefer Blondes* (Fox, 1953)

♥

Curtis: "Where did you learn to kiss like that?"
Monroe: "I used to sell kisses for the milk fund."
Curtis: "Tomorrow, remind me to send a check for $100,000 to the milk fund."
> —Tony Curtis responding to a kiss from Marilyn Monroe, *Some Like It Hot* (United Artists, 1959)

♥

"I have a message for your wife. Don't wipe it off. If she thinks that's cranberry sauce, tell her she's got cherry pits in her head."
> —Marilyn Monroe sending Tom Ewell back to his wife with a kiss, *The Seven Year Itch* (Fox, 1955)

♥

"Now I have kissed you through two centuries."
> —Laurence Olivier romancing Vivien Leigh into the nineteenth century, *That Hamilton Woman* (United Artists, 1941)

♥

"Just because I kiss you—does that make me your girl?"
   —Doris Day, *The Pajama Game* (Warner Bros., 1957)

♥

"Come on, give your mommy a big sloppy kiss."
   —Elizabeth Taylor to Richard Burton, *Who's Afraid of
      Virginia Woolf?* (Warner Bros., 1966)

♥

"I'd love to kiss you, but I just washed my hair."
   —Bette Davis to Richard Barthelmess, *The Cabin in the
      Cotton* (Warner Bros., 1932)

♥

"I'd just as soon kiss a Wookiee."
   —Carrie Fisher to Harrison Ford, *The Empire Strikes
      Back* (Fox, 1980)

♥

"That was restful. Again."
   —A Russian Greta Garbo allowing Melvyn Douglas to
      teach her the Western custom of kissing, *Ninotchka*
      (MGM, 1939)

♥

"When a woman kisses me, Louise, she has to take pot luck."
   —Van Heflin to Joan Crawford, *Possessed* (Warner
      Bros., 1947)

♥

"Don't tell me it's subversive to kiss a Republican."
   —John Lund romancing an Iowa congresswoman, Jean
      Arthur, *A Foreign Affair* (Paramount, 1948)

♥

"When a clumsy cloud from here meets a fluffy little cloud from there, he billowed toward her. She scurries away, and he scuds right up to her. She cries a little, and there you have your shower. He comforts her. They spark. That's lightning. They kiss. Thunder!"

    —Fred Astaire warming up Ginger Rogers, *Top Hat*
       (RKO, 1935)

Kissing Ditties

Kiss and hug
Kiss and hug,
Smack your sweetie
On the mug.

Kiss beneath the garden gate,
Kiss beneath a rose,
But the proper place to kiss a boy
Is right beneath the nose.

Pucker your lips
And close your eyes,
You're going to get
A big surprise!

Johnny and Susie
Sitting in a tree
K-I-S-S-I-N-G.
First comes love,
Then comes marriage,
Then comes junior
In a baby carriage.

Snuggle snuggle
Smooch and smack,
Kissing's fine
And that's a fact.

Kissing Facts & Trivia

Kissing Records

Longest kiss
It was performed in Chicago on September 24, 1984, by Eddy Leaven and Dolphin Chris. The kiss lasted seventeen days and 10.5 hours. At the conclusion of the event, the two celebrated with a kiss.

Longest kiss of life
Five members of the St. John Ambulance team of Australia performed mouth-to-mouth resuscitation, or the kiss of life,

for 315 consecutive hours. This kiss was started on August 27 and concluded on September 9, 1984. A total of 232,150 inflations took place, and the "patient"? Well, truth be told, it was actually a dummy.

Longest kiss underwater
Fuji TV captured the moment in Tokyo, Japan on April 2, 1980. The winning participants, Toshiaki Shirai and Yukiko Nagata, kissed underwater for 2 minutes, 18 seconds.

Most people kissed
A whopping 10,504 people were kissed by Alfred E. Wofram on August 19, 1990 in eight hours. This event took place in New Brighton, Minnesota during a medieval festival. Think about it: That's one kiss every 2.7 seconds.

Kissing Research

Number of men kissed before marriage
According to Dr. Joyce Brothers, the average American female will have kissed seventy-nine men before she says "I do."

Kissing prolongs your life
Kissing is known to reduce blood pressure and tension.

Kissing as a warning sign
The Marriage Guidance Council has found that the absence of kissing in a relationship is one of the very first signs that it is headed for a breakup.

Kissing helps your teeth

Research performed by several dentists has determined that kissing is good for your teeth. The act of kissing increases saliva flow, which in turn washes away food particles and lowers acid levels in the mouth. Therefore, kissing can help prevent plaque buildup and may lessen tooth decay.

Husbands, kiss your wives good-bye in the morning

This is the conclusion of a study conducted by Dr. Arthur Szabo and a group of German physicians and psychologists, in cooperation with insurance companies. They found that husbands who kiss their wives on the lips before leaving for work are happier, healthier, earn 20 to 30 percent more, live five years longer, have fewer accidents on the way to work, and begin the day with a positive attitude.

The "Pretty Woman" hypothesis

Sex therapist Martha Stein studied sixty-four call girls and their clients to better understand the association between deep kissing and emotional closeness of the middle class. While hiding in the bedroom, Stein observed 1,230 sexual encounters. Only 36 percent of the encounters included French kissing.

"Germ" and Kissing

In the 1950s, students from Baltimore City College analyzed glass slides that had been kissed to determine what germs are possibly passed in kissing. To their surprise, they discovered 278 colonies of bacteria. Fortunately, 95 percent of the transmitted colonies were found to be completely harmless.

The educated French kiss

According to the Kinsey Report, the French kiss is performed least in American culture by adult males whose education level is no greater than the eighth grade.

Buddhist Kisses

It was reported by surgeon C. M. Beadnell that a devout Buddhist on his final six-mile pilgrimage to Lhasa will kiss the ground more than thirty thousand times.

Kissing and AIDS

Though the AIDS virus can be found in saliva, there have been no recorded cases where kissing has resulted in transmission of the virus.

Kissing Games

Copy Kiss

While watching a movie or TV, you and your partner imitate the kissing scene.

The "Kissing Disease"

Dr. Alfred S. Evans coined the nickname "Kissing Disease" for a common virus known as mononucleosis because most cases are contracted through salivary interchange, as in kissing.

Celebrities on Kissing

Kisses of Mae West

In an interview with the Associated Press in 1968, Mae West confessed to never actually kissing a man during any of her performances on stage, and barely doing so in films. She stated: "I always felt that the look before the kiss was more important than the kiss itself. I figured it was better to fade out before the kiss and let the audience use its imagination."

Sharon Stone

Ms. Stone described her first kiss in a *Seventeen* magazine article in 1995. "I was in the basement of my parents' house. We were playing darts, and he kissed me. He kissed me, like, KISSED me! Like, wow! Not like your aunt kissing you, but like whoa! I was fifteen."

French Kiss Variations:

Tongue wrestle
•
Touch only the tips of each other's tongues
•
One licks the other's tongue
•
One sucks the other's tongue
•
Explore the roof of your partner's mouth
•
Lightly bite the other's tongue
•
Count their teeth with your tongue

Sandra Bullock

In the same *Seventeen* article, Ms. Bullock article talked about her first kiss as well. "Oh! This was so great! My cutie-pie neighbor boy kissed me through my bedroom window. He got his little best friend to go on all fours, and he stood on his pal's back to get up high enough. Isn't that sweet?"

Maurice Chevalier

Once asked why the French kiss friends of either sex on the cheek, he answered, "It is simply that we like to renew acquaintances, we Frenchmen. We may kiss a man we haven't seen for five years or a girl we haven't seen for five minutes."

Brad Pitt's Planned Peck

Brad Pitt described a kiss he had in fourth grade. "We actually made a plan at school to meet in her garage and kiss. It was like this little business deal. So I get there. I go right up to her. I kiss her. Then I ran home."

Bob Hope

When asked by a reporter to describe what it was like working in television opposite Lucille Ball, who at the time was president of Desilu, Hope responded, "I never thought I'd be kissing the president of a company on the lips."

More Bob Hope

A woman once kissed by Bob Hope asked him, "How did you ever learn to kiss like that?" "It comes natural, I guess," he replied. "I blow up all my own motorcycle tires."

Author James Joyce

After writing *Ulysses*, James Joyce was asked by a young man if he could kiss the hand that wrote such a great work. Joyce responded, "No," then added, "It did lots of other things, too."

Movie Kisses

First movie kiss

Performed in 1896 by May Irwin and John C. Rice for a thirty-second nickelodeon production by Thomas Edison entitled *The Kiss*.

Most kisses in any one movie

John Barrymore in Warner Brothers' 1926 production of *Don Juan*. A total of 191 kisses were recorded, with two-thirds going to the two costars, Mary Astor and Estelle Taylor.

Longest kiss in cinematic history

Regis Toomey and Jane Wyman performed a 185-second kiss in the 1941 release of *You're in the Army Now*. This kiss, which lasted a little more than three minutes, represented 4 percent of the movie's length.

Big screen kissing
The Screen Actors Guild in October of 1985 issued a policy statement that open-mouthed kissing could be "possibly hazardous work." This was in reaction to Rock Hudson kissing Linda Evans in the television show *Dynasty* shortly before he died of AIDS. Actors now must be told if their roles require open-mouthed kissing before being hired.

Little-Known Kissing Facts

Mr. Kiss
A Hungarian-American pharmacist, Max Kiss, is credited with combining chocolate with a laxative. He called it "Excellent Laxative," which was later shortened to Ex-Lax.

On-line kiss
The characters used to send a kiss to someone on the Internet are :*) If you look at it sideways, you will understand why.

Kissing tellers
A bank in Seattle posted a sign that read: "Don't kiss our girls—they're all tellers!"

The Anti-Kissing League
In 1909, a group of men from Kansas formed the Anti-Kissing League. These men viewed kissing as unhealthy and unnecessary and pledged to never again kiss their wives. The league shortly after disbanded.

Big red lips

It has been proved that during kissing and any acts of sexual arousal, both men and women's lips become swollen and red.

Kiss-me-quick

In 1850 England, a fashionable lady's hat which had no brim was named the "kiss-me-quick" hat because a man could access the woman's lips more quickly than when she wore a hat with a brim.

Kiss-me-if-you-can

The old-fashioned Danish hats worn by women with very prominent brims were called "kiss-me-if-you-can" hats. The name came into being because the brims posed a significant obstacle to any man attempting to kiss a woman who wore one.

Kissing fish

Called "kissing gourami," these are tropical fish with either pink or green-white color. They actually kiss their own kind on the mouth, and their kissing has been reported to last up to twenty-five minutes.

In the Mood to Smooch:

- An evening stroll
- Holding hands
- Watching a romantic movie
- Sitting together on a couch
- Listening to music
- Receiving flowers
- Candlelight
- Flirting
- Smiling

The kissing bug

A member of the *reduviodae* insect family, the "kissing bug" (*reduvius personatus*) can be found in homes, where it preys on bedbugs and other insects. Its name comes from the fact that the adult bugs will often bite humans around their mouth while sleeping.

Porcupine kiss
North American porcupines have their own unique courtship kiss. The male and female will nuzzle the tips of each other's noses, which is one of the very few places free of quills.

No-kissing zone
Deerfield, Illinois, has at least one claim to fame. The wives of Deerfield who drove their husbands to the train station were stopping traffic as they kissed their spouses good-bye. To relieve this traffic jam, the city created two zones fifty feet apart. They labeled the zones "Kissing" and "No Kissing."

Airport kissing delays
The New Orleans airport was experiencing problems with flights being delayed because of excessive "good-bye kissing" by outbound passengers. To keep flights on-time, the airport posted the sign: "Start kissing good-bye early so the plane can leave on time."

Kissing the blues
The famous Connecticut blue laws prohibited kissing—even by married couples—on Sundays and fasting days.

Illegal kissing
Don't kiss in public in Kuwait City, Kuwait. It is considered an immoral act and thus subject to a three-month jail term. If you are an expatriate, you might also be deported.

Washington, D.C. kissing
This city is known for its excessive social kissing. However, it reached an all-time high during the Carter years, when President Carter was several times reported kissing ladies without their consent.

Kiss of peace
The creation of the "kiss of peace" is credited to St. Paul. He instructed his followers to "Greet one another with a holy kiss" (Romans 16:16) during Christian services, baptism, confession, ordination, and communion.

Opera kissing dilemma
Sir Rudolf Bing, former opera administrator at New York's Metropolitan Opera, was faced with a flu epidemic spreading through the cast. His solution was to post a sign that read: "Confine your kissing to the irresistible" (*The Little Brown Book of Anecdotes*).

Kissing Customs

Mistletoe
The custom of exchanging a kiss under the mistletoe is not easy to pinpoint. The closest explanation comes from a Scandinavian myth. Balder, god of light and spring, dreamed his life was in danger. His mother, Frigga, goddess of love, therefore made Earth, Air, Fire, and Water promise they would not harm her son. She overlooked mistletoe, a parasitic plant which does not grow from any of the four elements. Loki, god of fire, was jealous of Balder, so he had him

slain with a dart of mistletoe. In her grief, Frigga decreed that mistletoe would never again be used as a weapon and promised to place a kiss on anyone who passed under it.

Today, this tradition can still be found in many countries. If a couple in love exchanges a kiss under the mistletoe, it is interpreted as a promise to marry. In France, the custom is reserved for New Year's Day: "Au gui l' an neuf" (Mistletoe for the New Year). Today, kisses can be exchanged under the mistletoe any time during the Christmas holiday season.

XXX

Those "Xs" at the bottom of letters to symbolize kisses originated in the Middle Ages. The illiterate would draw an "X" on the signature line of a contract when they couldn't sign their name and then kiss the contract to show sincerity. Eventually the "X" itself came to signify a kiss.

Blowing a kiss

The practice of blowing kisses to departing friends started during the Sargonic dynasty in Mesopotamia when pagan worshipers used this gesture to throw kisses to their pagan gods.

Kissing Superstitions

- ❤ Sneeze on Tuesday, you'll kiss a stranger.
- ❤ Kiss your elbow, and you'll change your sex.
- ❤ To protect yourself from lightning, make three crosses before you then kiss the ground three times. (German)
- ❤ Kiss over a gate, you'll have bad luck.
- ❤ If your nose itches, you'll be kissed by a fool.

- If a sitting woman and a standing man kiss each other, they'll quarrel.
- Before gambling, kiss the playing cards, and you'll have good luck. (French)
- If a bride doesn't cry when the groom first kisses her during the ceremony, their marriage will be unhappy.
- To relieve a toothache, kiss a donkey on his chops. (German)
- A kiss from a chimney sweep will bring you good luck.
- If you drop a book or piece of bread on the floor, you must kiss it when you pick it up to avoid bad luck. (Denmark, Germany)
- Kissing in a gondola under the Bridge of Sighs in Venice at sunset while the bells of the Campanile toll will bestow eternal love on the couple. (Italian)

Lip-Smacking Facts

What are lips?
Lips are a transition skin layer between the outer hair-bearing tissue and the inner mucous membrane. They have a high concentration of sensitive nerve endings, which explains why it is so enjoyable to have them lightly touched.

The perfect lips
Good news. There is no such thing. The "in" lip shape changes with each generation.

What shape lips are best for kissing?
Good news again. There is no best shape. It's how you use them that determines how good a kiss is.

A fix for chapped lips
Moisten lips with a warm washcloth until they feel soft. Rub a generous layer of petroleum jelly on them and allow it to set for three minutes. Now gently rub lips with the warm washcloth until all dry or loose skin is gone. Apply a creamy lipstick, then blot. Apply a second coat.

Lipstick
Lipstick is simply a combination of oil, pigment, and wax. The oil provides easy spreading and sticking. The pigment creates the color, and the wax is used to keep the lipstick's shape in the tube.

Lip gloss
Lip gloss is made of the same ingredients as lipstick. However, it has more oil and less wax.

Kissing Acronyms and Abbreviations

C.Y.K.
Consider yourself kissed

S.W.A.K.
Sealed with a kiss

Q.B.S.P.
Que besa sus pies (Spanish for "Who kisses your feet?")

K.I.S.S.
Keep it simple, stupid; or Keep it simple and stupid; or Keep it simple and sweet.

Q.B.S.M.
Que besa su mano (Spanish for "Who kisses your hand?")

Kissing Geography

Forehead . . . . Respect
Cheek . . . . Friendship and affection
Hand . . . . Homage
Foot . . . . Reverence and humility
Mouth . . . . Love

Kissing Terminology

First base
Getting a kiss from your date.

Philematology
The study of kissing.

Osculation
The act of kissing.

Osculogy
The science of kissing.

Osculogical
Something which pertains to kissing.

Maraichinage
Another word for deep kissing or French kissing. The word is derived from the Maraichins, a group of people who lived in Marais (a region in western France that borders on the Bay of Biscay). They were known to enjoy deep kissing.

Muckmouth
A slang word to describe a mouth which has become so dry that small bits of sticky saliva get caught in the corner of your mouth. When the mouth opens, the saliva creates a kind of web.

Lipograph
Invented by David Bowie in 1979. He sent a card with a lipstick print of his lips to a cosmetic firm publicist as a thank-you gesture. Inspired by the lip print, the publicist convinced eighty more celebrities to create "lipographs" to be auctioned off at a Save the Children Foundation benefit. The fund-raiser collected $16,000. The most expensive lipographs included Mick Jagger's for $1,600, and Marlene Dietrich's for $1,200.

Osculum
Latin for a kiss on the face or cheek between friends.

Basium
Latin for a kiss on the lips as a sign of affection.

Suavium or Savium
A Latin word meaning a kiss between the lips. Refers to a kiss between lovers.

Idiomatic Phrases

Hollywood kiss
To dismiss or get rid of someone ("Kiss off"). Used primarily on the East Coast, especially in New York City.

Kiss ass
To act submissive to someone in order to gain an advantage.

Kiss a cow
To verify the truth.

Kiss and be friends
To make peace.

Kiss and make up
To forgive and be friends again. It is believed to have originated in societies where a kiss of reconciliation precedes the handshake. Also used literally.

Kiss black betty
Drinking liquor to excess.

Kiss (something or someone) good-bye
To anticipate or experience the loss of something.

Kiss my ass
American and Canadian. A catchall phrase of profound contempt or an intensified negative. Dating back to 1860.

Kissing Games

Fire and Ice
The kissing version of tag. The person who is "it" is the ice prince or princess. He/she runs after the others trying to kiss them.
Once someone is kissed, that person must freeze in place until someone else can kiss and set him/her free.

Kiss and tell
Telling others about your romantic moments which should be kept secret. An article, book, interview, or film containing firsthand information that is confidential or embarrassing.

Kiss hands
Pay respect to someone.

Kiss it better
Give relief to a personal emotion or to a child's "boo-boo."

Kissing cousin
One of two or more things that are closely related.

Kiss my foot
Rubbish. Mostly an Australian and Canadian expression of the nineteenth and twentieth centuries.

Kiss my grits
An intensified negative. Same meaning as "drop dead" or "go jump in the lake."

Kiss my tail
A violently contemptuous retort of eighteenth- to-twentieth-century usage. Obsolete by 1960.

Kiss of death
Made famous by Alfred E. Smith in a speech describing William Randolph Hearst's support of Ogden Mills (1926). Also from Judas Iscariot's kissing of Christ in the great betrayal scene, thenceforth to any other callous betrayal. Applied to something that will ultimately be ruined.

Kiss my tuna
An all-purpose exclamation of rejection. Used primarily by "Valley Girls."

Kiss me, sergeant
World War I British army expression. A common jesting uttered after an officer had been somewhat serious about his rank. Was also said to the orderly sergeant in army camps after he commanded "lights out!"

Kiss of life
Mouth-to-mouth resuscitation.

Kiss off
To dismiss or get rid of something or someone, often rudely and curtly. To be forced to give up or regard as lost.

Kiss one's aircraft good-bye
To bail out. From the Royal Air Force air crews of World War II.

Kiss out
To be denied or cheated out of one's share of the profits.

Kiss the baby (babe)
To take a drink.

Kiss the book
To take an oath.

Kiss the canvas
Also "kiss the resin." A boxing term meaning to be knocked out.

Kiss the bottle
To drink liquor.

Kiss the claws
To salute.

Kiss the counter
To be confined to prison.

Kiss the cross
To be knocked out, as in boxing.

Kiss the dog
To pick a pocket while facing the victim.

Kiss the dust
To die, to be defeated, or to be overthrown.

Kiss the ground
To be humiliated or to be thrown off a horse.

Kiss the hare's foot
To be too late for meals. Probably meant that one coming to partake of the hare had no better chance but to kiss the hare's foot than to get something to eat.

Kiss the maid
To lose one's head in a guillotine; mid-eighteenth-century expression.

Kiss the gunner's daughter
To be tied to the ship's cannon and caned.

Kiss the porcelain god
To vomit.

Kiss the rod
To grovel.

Kiss the shilling
To be cheap (penny kisser).

Kisser wiper
A strike to the face.

New York kiss
To dismiss or get rid of someone. Used on the West Coast, especially in Los Angeles.

Play kissie
To be falsely friendly and flattering to another.

Kissing Drinks

A Widow's Kiss (Brandy drink)
1 oz. Five Star Brandy
1/2 oz. Benedictine
1/2 oz. Chartreuse (yellow)
1 dash bitters
Shake with ice and strain into cocktail glass.

Soul Kiss Cocktail (Vermouth)
1-1/2 tsp. orange juice
3/4 oz. dry vermouth

1-1/2 tsp. Dubonnet
3/4 oz. bourbon
Shake with ice and strain into cocktail glass.

Kiss-in-the-Dark (Vermouth)
3/4 oz. gin
3/4 oz. dry vermouth
3/4 oz. cherry-flavored brandy
Stir with ice and strain into cocktail glass.

Kiss the Boys Good-bye (Brandy)
3/4 oz. gin
1/2 egg white
3/4 oz. Five Star Brandy
juice of 1 lemon
Shake with ice and strain into cocktail glass.

Angel's Kiss (Pousse-cafe)
1/4 oz. Gremede Cacao (white)
1/4 oz. Five Star Brandy
1/4 oz. gin
1/4 oz. light cream
Pour ingredients carefully into pousse-cafe glass, in the order given, so they don't mix. (Pousse-cafes are sweet, striped drinks made by pouring a series of liqueurs in succession so that one floats on top of another.)

A Summer's Kiss (Mixed drink)
1 oz. Amaretto
3 oz. cranberry juice
Pour over ice into glass.

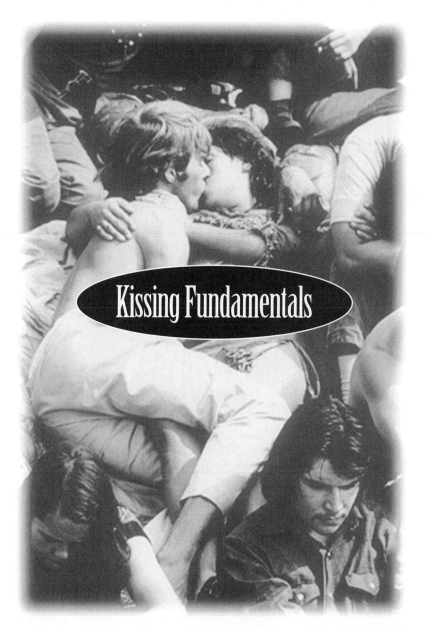

Kissing Fundamentals

Kissing Anatomy

E'VE ALL HAD disappointing kissing partners, including those who kiss hard enough to correct an overbite, or those who blow in your ear as if taking a Breathalyzer test. There are many variables to kissing, and they all interrelate—like anatomy. If all the variables aren't addressed, a kiss can fall apart and be disappointing. So here's an anatomy lesson on kissing. If your partner is a poor kisser, or you know of someone who is, take heart and read on.

Lips

Lips are the tools of kissing. It's tough to kiss without them. They ensure that the kiss comes across soft, warm, and moist. How your lips are positioned is critical to a successful romantic kiss. Contrary to popular thought, lips should not be puckered. This lip position causes the lip muscles to contract, creating a hard, wrinkled nodule. Kissing this is like kissing a doorknob.

The proper lip kissing position begins with relaxed lips. Now, part them just enough so they do not touch. Many kissers part their lips too far and their partner is left feeling as if they've been gummed by a carp. The lips should flare slightly outward to expose a hint of the inner lips. This inner lip is what gives a kiss its warm and moist quality. Think about how you hold your lips when drinking from a water fountain. That lip position is the favored kissing position.

It is important that your lips touch the lips of your partner softly. Smashing your partner's lips against their teeth is a very painful experience and reduces lip sensitivity. Men need to be particularly attuned to this problem since it is the most common complaint women have about men's kissing.

A deep kiss requires you to spread the lips farther apart, allowing the tongue to pass in and out of the mouth freely. Frequently the lips will roll back and expose the hazardous teeth, which may catch or pinch lips, or bite into gums, causing your partner undue pain. It may be difficult to concentrate simultaneously on lips, tongue, and teeth during a passionate kiss, however, do a check every once in a while to make sure your partner is having a good time.

Once you have the basic lip position mastered, don't get stuck in a puckering rut. Work together to come up with some unique hybrids such as kissing with your lower lips pouting, or with both pairs of lips so overcontracted that the two of you look like blowfish. Part of the fun of kissing is coming up with new variations or creating kisses that are special between the two of you.

One rumor that needs to be dispelled is that great kissing requires large lips. It has never been proved that one lip size is better for kissing than another. It is how people use their lips that determines how good a kisser they will be. Lip size is an attraction point, not a performance measure.

And a note on lips for women: It is a known fact that men are attracted to red lips. They find gleaming white even teeth framed with red lips to be very sexy and engaging. However, most do not like to kiss lipstick-clad lips because they wind up with lipstick all over their face. This is clearly a dilemma for women: to wear or not to wear. One piece of advice would be to wear red lipstick during the initial attraction stages, then switch to something else when the kiss seems imminent.

Mouth

The mouth is the cavity which houses the tongue, gums, and teeth. The lips form its external boundaries. It goes without saying that this area needs to be clean, polished, and odor-free for kissing. And any extraneous matter such as gum, chewing tobacco, sewing pins, and toothpicks needs to be removed. Nothing can dampen ardor more than a row of brown-stained, unkempt teeth, except for maybe bad breath. Bad breath can be caused by onions, peanuts, smoke, beer, and anything else your partner doesn't want to be tasting secondhand. (See "Kissing Anxieties" for a more detailed discussion.)

Every mouth also contains expectoration (spit), which needs to be controlled. Those who have experienced it know there's nothing worse than taking a face bath. Excessive saliva results from nervousness, excitement, or holding your breath, and can be avoided if you maintain a light suction while kissing. The light suction you use to drink from a straw is the same suction you use in kissing. It solves two problems: It prevents your saliva from escaping into your partner's mouth (or worse, down his or her face), and it forces you to breathe. You should also try to pause occasionally between kisses so you'll have time to swallow and catch your breath.

Tongue

The tongue is used during deep kissing or French kissing. It is bad form to sit for a kiss with your mouth open and tongue extended, as if in a dentist's chair, expecting your partner to do all the tongue work. On the other hand, too much tongue activity could leave your partner's tongue feeling as if it were caught in a food processor. A deep kiss is like two tongues slow dancing. This manner should be tender and endearing. The movements should be slow, smooth, rhythmic, and varied, with neither party forcing control. Try licking peanut butter off the end of your finger and notice the way your tongue maneuvers to remove it. This, and licking a popsicle are the closest comparisons to proper tongue motion in a deep kiss.

Concentrate on touching the more sensitive membranes on the walls of the mouth rather than focusing on the teeth.

Keep your tongue inside either mouth, and do not venture underneath your partner's tongue because more sensitive nerve endings are found on top of the tongue.

Taste

The mouth is used to sense taste, yet rarely do we consider this sense in kissing. A kiss can take on a whole new twist if you can find ways to titillate your tongue's sensory points. For instance, have you ever kissed someone after they've been sucking an ice cube or drinking hot chocolate? Try experimenting with different flavors of liqueurs, or coffee. Cover your teeth with honey, chocolate syrup, peanut butter, even toothpaste—something you know your partner likes—and have him or her kiss you until it's gone. It's also a great way to experiment with new tongue techniques. Keep in mind that the consistency of the food you pick is very important: oatmeal, scrambled eggs, or half-chewed popcorn have no visual appeal.

Eyes

When it comes to eyes and kissing, the question is always "Open or closed?" Most people kiss with their eyes closed. This is partly instinctive and partly because it is almost impossible to keep your partner in focus without going cross-eyed. Kissing closed-eyed also eliminates visual distractions, allowing you to concentrate on the kiss itself.

Marathon Kissonyms

Bundling
Prospecting
Fool Around
Submarine Race
Giraffing
Smooching
Give a Hot House
Suck Face
Grazing
Turtlenecking
Go into a Huddle
Swappin' Spit
Lip Push-ups
Lip Mingling
Ticklin' Tonsils
Moontanning
Making Out
Tongue Trekking
Mugging
Attend Parkology
Molar Mashing
Tongue Wrestle
Neckfest
Catching Monk
Mug Muzzle
Whoopee Warm-Up
Necking
Chew Face
Petting Party
Nuzzling
Explore the Waists
Play Post Office
Petology
Fling Woo
Snout Friction

Pierre Maranda, a Canadian anthropologist, claims 97 percent of women keep their eyes closed when kissing, compared with only 30 percent of men. Maranda's percentages are subject to debate, but it is true that women more than men kiss with their eyes closed. Women close their eyes to fantasize during the moment. Men tend to keep them open to heighten their own desire.

The moment of eye closure is important. If you close too early, you can lose your aim. You should close your eyes right after the head tilts and just before the lips touch to avoid a nose crash.

Those who prefer kissing with their eyes open reason that gazing into their partner's eyes makes the kiss more intense, or they want to see the effect they are having on their partner. If you're a closed-eye kisser and have an open-eye kissing partner, don't worry. Everything that close will be out of focus. The brain also interprets nearby faces as erotic, so you'll appear sexier to your kissing partner.

"Wide-eyed" kissing has some drawbacks; your partner looks like a Cyclops unless you're willing to endure the necessary eye strain to keep focus. And if one of you chooses to close your eyes, the other is left gazing into a pair of eyelids. Other than the two of you being myopic, the easier solution is for everyone simply to kiss with their eyes closed.

Kissing with eyes closed has a benefit: It creates another kissable facial surface—the eyelid. Most enjoy being kissed there. However, be aware that it can pose a problem for some contact-lens wearers. Pressure on their eyelids can be painful. Also, women who wear considerable eye makeup may not enjoy being kissed on the eyelids either. They fear having their eye shadow smeared across the rest of their face.

Ears

The ears can be a wonderful stimulation point to kiss because of their sensitivity. However, far too often they get abused by people speaking too loud, blowing too hard, or planting a kiss so wet that it sends the recipient sprinting for a Q-tip. Unless your partner is hard of hearing, you should never speak directly into an ear. Whispering is great because it sends small short bursts of air directly into the recipient's ear, creating tickling and/or shivering sensations that most find stimulating and enjoyable.

Blowing deliberately into someone's ear is a very popular, though tricky, form of seduction. Never form a seal between lips and ear, or you can cause significant inner ear damage. Blowing should be light and sustained, as if you are blowing on hot soup or coffee. And never blow into someone's ear if you have something in your mouth.

If you want to use your tongue for added excitement around the ear, for goodness sake, don't dribble. Drenching someone's ear is a major kissing *faux pas*. The suction technique described earlier will prevent any saliva buildup, as will pausing to swallow.

Try lightly nibbling on your partner's earlobes, tracing the ear with your nose, or lightly touching all over the ear using one of your fingers. Remember that any noise close to the ears will be greatly magnified (humming could sound like an air raid alert), so keep all sound to a minimum.

Inhaling is an appealing alternative to blowing into your partner's ear. Put your lips near the ear and lightly inhale through your mouth the same way you suck on a straw. The recipient gets a tingling sensation.

If you treat the ears properly during a kiss, you can heighten the experience. And don't linger on the ear for too long. It's like force-feeding chocolate chip cookies: Too much of a good thing diminishes its value, but a little taste leaves you hungry for more.

Height

Couples are generally not of equal height. Most of the time the man is taller. Psychologically, men prefer this height difference when performing a standing kiss because it gives them a sense of control. He feels as if he will be able to sweep her into his strong manly arms, look down into her upturned eyes, cup her chin in his fingers, and then bend over her face and plant his virile lips on her sweet, submissive mouth. If the heights are reversed, and the man is lower, he feels his physical mastery is gone. If you are a woman who likes the man to take the lead in kissing, keep this fact in mind.

If the heights are severely unequal, one head must fall way back and the other bend forward in order to perform a standing kiss. With the average head weighing eight to ten pounds, holding this position is a significant strain on the neck. Assuming the two of you aren't far enough along in your relationship to assume a horizontal position, try finding a kissing position that reduces the height disparity. Have the taller partner sit or lean on something, or have the shorter one find a stair or high-heeled shoes to stand on. Or try sitting down.

Hands

The hands' rule in kissing is: "If it's traditionally covered by underwear, don't touch it." Now, this rule need not be applicable if the two of you are "familiar" with one another. But generally speaking, a kiss can be ruined if hands navigate their way onto controversial body parts. The conservative approach is always to keep your hands above your partner's neck or around the waist. Some hands suggestions are: caressing the back of their neck or cheeks, running fingers through their hair and/or lightly pulling it, clasping your partner's hands in yours, and playing with the ears.

For those of you with a more southerly final destination in mind, there is an acceptable alternative for your hands. Start touching a neutral area, then when the two of you become comfortable kissing, slowly begin moving one hand toward your goal. This signals your partner of your eventual target. If you're on the receiving end and do not like where your partner's hands are heading, stay calm and continue kissing, but lightly take the guilty hand and move it somewhere more appropriate. You may have to repeat this, but after a few times, he or she should get the picture. If your partner continues groping, take more aggressive action, such as leaving.

Once the hands are situated satisfactorily, focus on hand movement. The person in your arms wants to be caressed. Gently touch and stroke him or her in an affectionate manner. Tickling, poking, and quick darting movements are inappropriate and unappealing, as is focusing on one spot and rubbing it till the skin becomes raw or desensitized. The hands should continually search out new areas, keeping your partner alert and aroused, and forcing you to be creative.

Nose

The nose is the one obstacle that can prevent you from coming in for a direct landing on your partner's lips. Often we find ourselves head-tilting from side to side trying to settle in for a kiss. This nose-juking can be downright frustrating and can kill the magic. Informal research has uncovered that most people instinctively tilt to the right. So let's just make a pact here and now. From here on, everyone tilt to the right and eventually the nose crash problem will disappear.

And during a kiss, be alert to the location of your partner's nose. Make certain it's not obstructed or squashed. Kissing and rubbing noses is a perfectly acceptable practice. Exploring the inside of the nose with your tongue or trying to bite nose hairs are definite no-no's. And don't even think about kissing if you have a runny nose. Your partner could catch your cold (or your runoff).

Scent

Kissing is about as close as you can get to another person. Therefore, your partner is going to pick up your scent. Obviously, bad breath and body odors will probably ruin an otherwise effective kiss. Chemistry between two people can be heightened if each is attracted to the other's scent. Many, therefore, will use perfumes, body lotions, and shampoos to enhance their natural body scent.

Old folklore suggests that women begin a kiss with their lips parted so the man may be intoxicated by the delicious odor emanating from her mouth. Perhaps this tale is the reason many women have touched the corners of their mouth ever so lightly with perfume to give it a faint fragrant odor.

Men are known to be attracted to the odor of a woman's hair. (Research also found that the smell most exciting to men is pumpkin pie...Go figure.) Women can be attracted to the scent of a man's shirt. History with a certain scent can have a lot to do with an attraction. For example, if the woman is wearing the same perfume the man's mother used to wear, or the man smokes the same cigar that the woman's father used to smoke, this can signal fond memories and further attract a kissing partner.

Don't forget the powerful sense of smell when trying to initiate or receive a kiss.

Breathing

Do it. For whatever reason, some prefer to refrain from breathing during a kiss. This causes lightheadedness and increases saliva production. Breathing lets you kiss longer without having to break for air. Try breathing lightly through your nose, or learn to pull back to light lip touching so you can catch some air.

Be sensitive to your partner's breathing as well. If your partner breaks away from your kiss gasping for air, chances are your kissing obstructs his or her breathing. Also, if you partner is breathing through the mouth, you're probably guilty of nose-smashing. Be especially alert if you're kissing an asthmatic. These people have a hard time breathing even when not being kissed. Take extra precautions to give them some room.

Variation

A woman once confided to me that she had been kissed by a human typewriter. Beginning at the left ear, he planted a row of kisses over to her right ear, then, at the imaginary ring of the carriage return, he shot back to the left ear and started all over again.

Kissing should never be a programmed set of movements. It should be spontaneous and unpredictable. Repeated lip-to-lip kissing becomes boring and can cause lip chapping. Try lip nibbles, tongue whips, nose brushes, or any other creative modifications you can come up with. (See "A Listing of Kisses," page 153.) Varying your kisses keeps your partner attentive and can result in longer kisses.

Timing

Don't prolong a kiss if your partner wants to stop. Ending a kiss while you both want more is safer than suffering the embarrassment of having your partner ask you to get off his or her face. Likewise, don't launch into a passionate kiss at the very beginning. It can set your partner on the defense or, worse, can turn him or her off completely. Let the intensity and duration of your kisses grow until the time feels appropriate to move on to more involved kissing.

Position

The key is finding a position that doesn't cause limbs to fall asleep or muscles to stretch into unnatural postures. Allow enough distance between you to prevent the compression of body parts but not so much space that it is difficult to touch the lips. Avoid kissing with an obstacle between the two of you, such as a fence, table, or stick shift of a car. It is also bad form to force your partner on to his or her back first. Again, experiment to find new and creative kissing positions. (See "Kissing Embraces," page145.)

DEEP KISSONYMS

FRENCHING
SPIT SWAPPING
TONGUE TALK
HOT TONGUING
SWAPPING SPIT
TONGUE TO TONGUE
LIP SUSHI
SWEETY SMOOCH
TONGUE WRESTLING
MARAICHINAGE
TASTE BUD DINNER
TONGUE TUMBLE
JOWL SUCKING
TASTE BUD THIRST
TONSIL DIVING
SOUL KISS
TASTE BUD PROJECTILE
TONSIL SWABBING
SPIN CYCLE
TONGUE DANCING
TONSIL SWALLOWING
SPIT SAMPLING
TONGUE SANDWICH
TONSIL BOXING

Strength

Men generally are stronger than women, so a woman can be frightened easily when a man is too physical. Men should never pin a woman down, constrain her movements, or put her in a hold that she can't easily break out of. It is the man's responsibility to make certain that the woman always feels safe and secure in his company.

Conclusion

These are the basic elements of a well executed kiss. As you probably discovered, kissing involves all your senses: sight, because visual attraction is important; sound, because ears are the receivers of inspiration; smell, because it creates chemistry; touch, because it is the reason to kiss someone at all; and taste, because in more ways than one, it is everything in kissing.

It is important that you make a careful and honest evaluation of each element to identify any shortcomings in your kissing technique. Once the errors are corrected, and the proper method put to practice, the next step is to develop a kissing style unique to your own personality.

The First Romantic Kiss

A SULTRY MELODY is heard over a crackling fire which illuminates a fashionable penthouse suite. A tall, handsome man grasps a shapely, scantily clad woman in his arms. A seemingly endless stream of longing glances ensues until the two slowly close their eyes and move their mouths toward one another. At last, their lips touch to a crash of cymbals and bursting fireworks. Their first kiss was perfect.

Unfortunately, first romantic kisses like this one only seem to happen in movies, soap operas, or in the imagination of some woebegone romantic. The truth about kissing someone romantically for the first time is that more often than not it's an awkward, blundering affair consumed with clumsy touching, incorrect nose placement, and poorly pursed lips.

A first kiss with someone you care about can be an incredibly exhilarating experience when performed correctly. However, few of us inherited the "James Bond genius" for knowing where, when, and how to kiss someone into spellbinding submission. All too often the "first kiss jitters" cause the kiss to be put off or delayed too long, and the opportunity vanishes.

What goes into making a first romantic kiss successful? This chapter is committed to answering this very question. And for those of you who want to better understand the transition from basic kissing into "French kissing" or deep kissing, you'll find answers and advice on this as well. So, let's begin by talking about some of the successful ways to set up a first kiss.

Romantic first kisses should only be exchanged between people who care about each other. So, assuming you've chosen the right person, you also must determine the proper place and time. If your partner feels the place is inappropriate, it can spell immediate disaster. Most people, for example, don't like kissing or being kissed in public. This is commonly referred to as a "P.D.A." (public display of affection). A P.D.A. also includes kissing when there is an audience: friends, family, or coworkers. A first romantic kiss really needs to take place somewhere special.

It's also hard to concentrate on kissing in an atmosphere where the more immediate concern is safety. For instance, leaning in for a smooch while driving a car or preparing to disengage from a ski lift. A successful location for a first kiss is anywhere you are able to concentrate wholly on your partner. To that end, it should be private and comfortable, perhaps with romantic lighting and/or a pretty view.

An element of kissing which seems to receive little thought is temperature. If the two of you are suffering from heat, it is a pretty sure bet that more concern is going to perspiration stains and body odor than to romance. In a cooler environment, however, a convincing argument can be made for getting close to your partner, either in an effort to get warm or to demonstrate caring for the other person's obvious discomfort. So consider turning down the thermostat. Then, at the first sign of goose bumps, come to your partner's aid.

As for timing, there are obvious moments when it's best to observe restraint. It's no fun to kiss when you're preoccupied with a time constraint such as an appointment with a $100-an-hour plumber or dealing with a nearing deadline at the office. If your potential partner is on the phone reciting a sequence of numbers that might win a free trip to the Virgin Islands, don't interrupt. What if, when President Bush was saying "Read my lips," Barbara Bush was trying to kiss them? The right time is when there is time to do it right.

Okay, we've got the right person, the perfect place, and the proper time. The execution of the first kiss is imminent. How do you make sure you don't blow it?

The biggest blunder most make with a first kiss is rushing. They approach at lightning speed with an intensely passionate first kiss thinking it will excite or overwhelm their partner. Wrong. Kissing is not like an Olympic

Kissing Games

Kissing under the Mistletoe

This game is played primarily around the Christmas holiday season. The official rules are if the woman is caught standing under a sprig of mistletoe, any man has the right to kiss her, peremptorily, without asking her permission or begging her pardon. The man can seize hold of the girl with impunity and kiss her to his heart's content without being socially ostracized for it. Today the rules have changed a bit.

event where speed wins the medal. So avoid zooming in with your mouth wide open, tongue at the ready, and crazed looking eyes.

A first kiss should always begin slowly and tentatively. You then build from there. One idea is to begin with an exploratory touch of the lips. This permits both of you the opportunity to decide whether or not to proceed. If one of you feels reluctant, the situation is recoverable with minimum embarrassment to either party. A slow and easy approach ferrets out your partner's style and technique while at the same time demonstrating respect for them. You also establish a kind of trust which leads to a more relaxed and comfortable atmosphere. And finally, a slower pace lets this special kiss last even longer. And isn't that the whole idea?

Another stumbling block with a first kiss is overaggressiveness. Delivering a deep kiss too soon, impersonating an octopus, or removing clothing with your teeth are all overly aggressive actions. Any time you display dominance over the situation with the aim being self-gratification rather than pleasing your partner, this is overaggressive behavior. A woman kissing a man for the first time leaves lipstick traces all over his face. She doesn't care that he looks like Bozo the clown. She is more interested in covering

Kissing Dos

- Make sure your breath is clean.
- Feel free to make the first move if the other partner is shy and can't "read your lips" well enough to know you want to be kissed.
- Compliment your kissing partner. It is encouraging. Any praise goes a long way toward getting your partner to work on their technique.
- Say "no" if you begin to feel the kissing is getting out of control or leading toward more intimacy than you are interested in.

surface area. A man, so self-consumed by his pleasure doesn't comprehend that he is obstructing the only two openings through which his partner exchanges oxygen—the nose and mouth. She is breathless—but it's not from euphoria. Remember, there are two of you kissing, and both of you should be participating and enjoying. The synergism of two far outweighs a solo act.

The First Kiss Process

With some of the first-kiss basics covered, let's move on to successfully executing the kiss. A series of steps has been designed to help you. These steps were created with an air of conservatism. After all, the goal is to deliver an impressive first kiss and avoid any awkward moments. Please note, however, that there is no singular right way to kiss someone for the first time, and no guarantee is being given here.

Let's walk through the steps, expanding on each step's relevance in the first-kiss process. A flow chart of the steps is available for those of you who are more technically minded on page 88.

1 *Decision to Kiss*
You know you want to kiss someone because you have been thinking about it for most of the evening. Well, unless your potential kissing partner is a mind reader, nothing is going to happen if you don't take some initiative. So make the decision and go forward with the next step.

2 Physical Contact

Take a reading on your potential partner's interest in the idea. You can do this with a gentle touch. Try either holding the person's hand, walking arm-in-arm, sitting close, offering a neck massage, or gently kissing the back of that person's hand. If you sense disapproval, smile, drop whatever you may be holding, and proceed with light conversation. (You have not yet put yourself in an embarrassing position, and you now have time to reevaluate the situation and perhaps try again later.)

3 Establish a Position

If he or she is responding positively to your physical contact, the next step is positioning yourself so that you'll feel comfortable kissing your partner. In most situations, the optimal position is face-to-face with shoulders squared and body height equal, either standing or sitting. It is preferable not to hold on to your partner. However, if you choose a hold, make sure it's nonthreatening. Your partner should never feel confined or restrained.

4 Eye Contact

The eyes are capable of giving great insight into how your future kissing partner is feeling. Try to establish eye contact. If your eyes are not met, or eye contact is broken quickly, this is a signal to retreat. If the eye contact is sustained, move on to the next step.

5 Move in Closer

You are comfortably positioned, and you have strong eye contact. Now is the time to move in for the kiss. This is the final checkpoint prior to kissing. As you move in, pause slightly before touching the lips to see if your partner is also moving forward. This pause should take place around the time your partner's nose falls out of focus and your head begins to tilt in order to avoid a nose collision. The other party ought to make an ever-so-slight advance to let you know he or she is in agreement. If this doesn't happen, you may continue to the next step or take the conservative approach—draw back and reexamine your partner's eyes.

Kiss

With a positive response from your partner, it is now time to approach for a romantic mouth-to-mouth kiss. Slowly and thoughtfully, ease forward until the lips gently touch. Don't complicate the situation by bringing your tongue into play.

Stop

As the initiator of the kiss, you should also be the one to end it. It is considered bad form to have the receiving partner break away. Do not be abrupt, and in no way signal the end to further kissing. Simply pull back and observe your partner's eyes. If you move forward to continue with the kissing, and your partner does not, this is a sign that perhaps he or she doesn't feel any chemistry. In this situation, it is advised that you stop kissing.

Kissing Games

Seven Minutes in Heaven

A more sophisticated version of Spin the Bottle. You and the person the bottle points to go into a closet where you make out for seven minutes.

Flow of a First Kiss

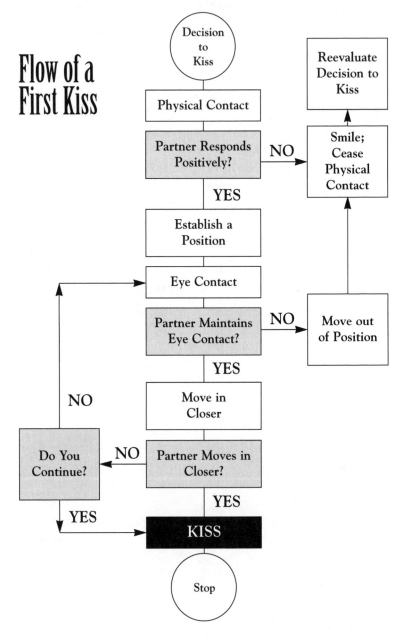

Decision to Kiss

Physical Contact

Partner Responds Positively? — **NO** → Smile; Cease Physical Contact → Reevaluate Decision to Kiss

YES

Establish a Position

Eye Contact

Partner Maintains Eye Contact? — **NO** → Move out of Position

YES

Move in Closer

Partner Moves in Closer? — **NO** → Do You Continue? — **NO** → Eye Contact / **YES** → KISS

YES

KISS

Stop

These steps are merely guidelines to performing a first roman-tic kiss. Establishing physical contact could mean hugging, sharing ice cream, reading a menu together, or holding hands. You can get a quick "willingness" reading by asking your partner to dance with you to a slow song. How about inviting the person over to your place to help cook a meal? (If the kitchen is small enough, you can't help but make physical contact.) And that cliché move of stretching your arms only to land your arm around their shoulders may be cornball, but it sends a signal and usually works. Adapt these guidelines to suit your own personality and style.

A First Deep Kiss

Now that you have successfully performed a first kiss, it's time for paydirt: the notorious French kiss, or deep kiss. French kissing doesn't start and stop abruptly. This type of kissing begins much like knocking on someone's front door. The way you knock can determine whether you are invited inside. With your partner relaxed and responding affirmatively to your kisses, try parting your lips. Unless he or she pulls back, you can then try gently touching the person's lips with your tongue. If you meet resistance, reel in your tongue, bring your lips back together, and resume kissing as you were earlier.

Don't interpret resistance as an unequivocal rejection. It's just a decision to hold off for now. Many women have a per-sonal rule of not deep kissing during the first kiss. They want to get to know their partner better. And, don't aggravate the situation by asking for an explanation. It leaves you wide open for some unflattering truth, like "I couldn't continue because your breath reminds me of three-day-old cat food," or "The weather is here, I wish you were beautiful." Holding off will also increase your chances of having a next time.

On the flip side, if your partner responds to your "knocking" by parting his or her lips, consider this gesture an invitation for your tongue to enter the mouth, and go on in, gradually. It is poor technique to thrust your tongue headlong into the mouth at a speed that could break the sound barrier or dental work. Proceed slowly and tentatively. The tongue contains very sensitive nerve endings. A light touch can cause quite a sensation.

The initiator now moves the tongue forward only as far as is necessary to meet the recipient's tongue. Once the tongues meet, each should massage the other in a tender caress. (See "Kissing Anatomy," page 67.) When the two of you begin to feel comfortable kissing this way, you can return to simple kissing or advance to more involved "hot tonguing." The conclusion of a deep kiss should not be abrupt—a soft, smoochy ending is far preferable to a dismissive smack. Perhaps two or more little kisses after the "big one" signals a graceful finish.

Proper deep kissing has its own etiquette. Basically, there are three rules:

1 Account for Your Own Expectoration (Spit)

When you're nervous or excited you produce more saliva. To avoid sending backwash into your partner's mouth, or drooling on yourself, maintain a continuous light suction while kissing. Also, periodically break away from the kiss to swallow and catch your breath.

2 Avoid Gagging Your Partner

Your tongue should be a welcome guest rather than a rude intruder in your partner's mouth. Do not wander down your partner's throat. Retching and/or choking sounds by your partner are a sign your tongue has gone too far.

3 Don't "Over-French"

Lengthy deep kisses can be as tedious as listening to a record skip. And your lips start to feel like raisins. Orchestrate your kissing encounter with an artful combination of deep and simple kisses to create crescendos and diminuendos. Variation keeps your partner attentive.

A final thought on a first romantic kiss: After the first kiss, the two of you enter into a whole new relationship, with a new set of rules. Future kisses will never be quite like the first, so make every effort to treat this event as a special, unpredictable moment and strive to create a fabulous memory.

"The dearest remembrance will still be the best. Our sweetest memorial the first kiss of love."

LORD BYRON

♥

Kissing Etiquette

THERE IS A LOT of confusion and misinformation about the etiquette of kissing. For example, when should a cheek be offered instead of the lips? Should hands be kissed, and if so, how? Must all good-night kisses be unconditionally accepted? Since few know the answers, most have taken the "If it feels good, do it" approach. Thus, unknown homely relatives are stealing kisses, good-night kisses are being foisted upon unwilling recipients, and perfect strangers are trying to kiss innocent babies. Clearly, it is time for some lines to be drawn.

Help has finally arrived. This part of the book lays out the socially acceptable practices for kissing. To begin, there are six basic points of kissing etiquette which make up the Code of Kissing Courtesy. Following the code will help you feel more comfortable about kissing and will put your partner at ease.

1 Don't Kiss and Tell

This is the first and oldest rule of kissing. It is also the one most often broken. Sharing with others a long and much embellished description of a kiss shared with a partner shows thoughtlessness toward them. It also can mar unfairly their reputation. Kiss, but then don't advertise.

2 Don't Overkiss

In the stock market, the more shares of stock issued, the less each share's value becomes. The same holds true of kisses. Stop short (but not abruptly). This strategy will almost certainly leave your partner wanting more and win you a future kissing opportunity.

3 Don't Kiss if You Are Infectious

If you're not feeling well, have a cold, mononucleosis, an open sore, or any other infectious condition, for heaven's sake, inform your partner and refrain from kissing.

4 Don't Laugh After a Kiss

It's disturbing to hear a partner break into laughter immediately after a serious kiss. It can hurt feelings and break a romantic mood.

5 Don't Kiss Unless You Want To

Kiss someone because you want to, not because you feel obligated. Giving a kiss out of pity, compensation for buying dinner, or merely to end an evening quickly are all poor reasons to kiss; you mislead the recipient. If you feel you must do something, that's what cards, flowers, and telephones are for.

6 Don't Kiss and Grope

Are you kissing just to kiss, or kissing as a prelude to something else? If you're "just kissing," then your hands shouldn't be taking an inventory of your partner's body parts. Groping hands not only distract and presume, they're annoying.

Handling the Situation

Some common kissing situations or circumstances baffle us. Here are recommendations on how best to handle them and keep your kissing on its proper course:

The Mouth or Cheek?
Kissing on the mouth should be reserved for spouses, lovers, close family members, and very, very close friends. An inappropriate mouth kiss is awkward and can make the partner of the recipient jealous and/or furious. When in doubt, kiss the cheek: and go for their right one, which is where most go.

Hand Kissing
Hand kissing, though popular in Europe, is not commonly practiced in America. Regardless, if you feel the urge to do it, there are some social conventions to be followed. Only men should perform hand kisses. Men should not kiss the hand of an unmarried woman; hand kissing is reserved for married women only. The lips of the man should never actually touch the skin of the woman's hand. And finally, don't kiss the palm of a lady's hand; this sends all the wrong signals.

If the woman wants her hand kissed, she should extend her hand slightly higher than she would to receive a handshake with the palm down rather than open. A man who is not used to this gesture is better off shaking the woman's hand lightly than attempting to kiss it.

Kissing Babies

It is rude to kiss someone else's infant without permission. Chances are the parents have been working very hard to keep their baby healthy. They do not appreciate potential germ-carrying individuals near their baby without an invitation. If you are invited to be near their baby, at least make sure your kiss is quick and germ-free.

Children and Kissing

Children should only kiss people they really like. They should not be forced to kiss anyone else. Adults should appreciate this because children up to a year old are major carriers of germs. It's better to encourage your child to use adult behavior and hug or extend a hand for a handshake.

Kissing Don'ts:

- Put on lipstick if you think you're about to get kissed.
- Make out in public. Kissing is meant to be a private affair.
- Chew gum and kiss at the same time.

Kissing Family Members

Some family members love to kiss each other even when only a few hours may have elapsed between visits. Others never kiss, or only kiss after a very long absence. Regional variations, family background, and lineage make it hard to establish rules or guidelines. The best recommendation is to observe and then go with the flow.

Woman-to-Woman Kissing

One woman kissing another on the cheek as a greeting is rather commonplace these days. Tradition dictates that the elder of the two women decides whether to kiss or shake hands (if you know which one that is). If the age difference is negligible, either party can initiate. Women usually head for the cheek and simulate any number of kissing gestures and sounds to avoid smearing lipstick. Women kissing each other on the lips is still socially unacceptable except between mother and daughter.

Man-to-Man Kissing
Magic and Isaiah do it; European men have been kissing cheeks for generations. Most American men, however prefer a handshake or a hug.

Kissing in Public
The taboo on public kissing has relaxed some over the last twenty-five years. Nevertheless, public kissing or P.D.A.'s (public displays of affection), when performed, should be short and sweet. Aerobic tongue work and probing hands are public kissing no-no's. When amour strikes in public, look around till you find a private spot.

Kissing at Airports
Airports or other ports of call like train and bus stations send emotions racing more than other public places because people are either parting or reuniting. A short, sweet kiss usually won't satisfy the moment.

If you can, get all your emotional leave-taking done in the

car. If you insist on staying together until the final boarding call, at least find a semiprivate spot away from the crowd to kiss, and keep it brief. If someone is arriving, try to hold off until you reach the car before giving a passionate welcome or at least move out of the way of those who are trying to dis-embark.

Kissing at the Front Door

Let's assume your evening went well, that proper etiquette reigned, and the two of you now stand at the front door. The general front door rule for a first kiss is to keep the kiss short. Men, don't linger around like a cat waiting to be let in after-ward.

The Good-night Kiss

Without a doubt, the first good-night kiss is the most awk-ward kiss. Men feel obligated to attempt it; women feel oblig-ated to comply. Therefore, most of us dispense or receive a first good-night kiss out of ritual or simply habit. The result all too often is a quick peck on tightly sealed lips.

The good-night kiss should never be the first romantic kiss between the two of you because it signals the end of the evening! If you really think about it, the good-night kiss is really a silly tradition. The best recommendation on this kiss is not to worry about it. It can always be skipped if your good-bye is handled correctly. Try sincerely thanking your date for the evening and then saying good night. After you have shared a romantic kiss with your partner, good-night kisses are acceptable and preferable.

Clothing

Believe it or not, clothing can play an adverse role in kissing. Loosely woven garments can snag while fashions with tassels, beads, and other accoutrements can get caught or even blind your partner. Also be wary of soft knits that may be allergens. Before dressing, keep these points in mind.

Jewelry

Women, think twice about wearing protruding pins and sharp earrings that can skin noses, scratch skin, or tear clothing. Men, watch your watch. It can catch and get tangled in hair or clothing.

Eyeglasses

For the record, men *do* make passes at women who wear glasses, and vice versa. Anyway, perfect vision isn't necessary for great kissing because most of us kiss with our eyes closed. Glasses only become a kissing issue when both of you wear them. You need to work together to find the right position to prevent eyewear from crashing. Another option is for both of you to take off your glasses.

Glasses can even become a great prop for kissing. Remove your partner's glasses gently and seductively to signal that a kiss is on its way. If you wear glasses, remove them as a gesture of willingness.

Gum

If you're caught with gum in your mouth, you have two choices—discreetly remove it or swallow it.

Breath Mints

Timing is everything. You can look presumptuous popping a mint in your mouth seconds before moving in for a kiss, or excusing yourself only to come back with Certs breath. Chew breath mints after you eat something pungent, then politely offer one to your partner as well. Don't try to hide the fact that you've taken one. (See "Kissing Anxieties," page 106 for more on breath control.)

Regional Variations

Kissing customs vary from one region to the next in this country. People from large cities are more accustomed to social kissing. Those from Washington, D.C., New York, California, and the South often greet their most casual acquaintances with kisses. Midwesterners and westerners tend to be reserved, indulging far less in social kissing. It is best to take a moment and observe when you are in a new area before exercising your pucker.

Kissing Around the World

Be aware that many countries have quite different attitudes and responses toward kissing. Here's a sample list:

French—Will kiss you twice—once on each cheek—or three times in some regions.

Belgians—Often kiss you three times.

Chinese—For the most part do not kiss in public.

West Africans—Feel repulsed to see tourists kissing.

Austrians—Are famous for kissing on the hand.

Laplanders—May kiss the mouth and the nose at the same time.

Indonesians—Kiss only the cheek.

Japanese—Before their contact with the West, did not practice kissing.

Germans—Have thirty words for kissing; for example, *Nachkus* is a kiss given to make up for kisses that were overlooked.

Greeks—Like to kiss hello on the mouth; even male friends do it.

Finlanders—Consider mouth-to-mouth kissing obscene.

Arapeshians—According to Margaret Mead, touch lips together and draw each other's breath in.

Eskimos, Malaysians, Polynesians, Balinese—Primarily rub noses as their form of a kiss.

Indians—Fairly recently lifted a ban on actual mouth contact in movies.

Arabs and Hindus—Consider kissing an erotic act.

Turn-ons & Turnoffs

HEN IT COMES to the subject of kissing, everyone seems to have a definite opinion about what turns them on and off. There seems to be very little gray area for most. What is curious is that a turn-on for you could be a turnoff for your partner. For this reason, you may find the same thing appearing under both categories.

The following is a general listing of kissing turn-ons and turnoffs. The lists are fairly comprehensive, but you may have unique additions of your own. Sit down with your kissing partner and go through the lists. It will be both fun and informative.

Kissing Turn-ons

Tongue—Since most people like deep kissing.

Eyes closed

Perfume

Lipstick—Most men are attracted to a lipstick-framed mouth.

Tenderness

Candlelight

Suspense—Causing pleasant excitement in anticipation of the eventual kiss.

A slow build—To a deep kiss.

Soft voice—Whispering, or speaking softly near the ear.

Soft lips

Toe kisses

Wrapped in arms—While being kissed.

Spontaneity—When it comes to trying a new kiss or embrace.

Hair tugs

Shapely lips

Tongue sucking—Having your tongue lightly sucked by your partner.

Confidence—When approaching someone to kiss him or her.

Hearing the other's breathing—Especially if it becomes short and excited.

Sighs and moans

Deep breathing

Facial hair—Women either love it or hate it.

Light nibbling—Lightly biting their lower lip.

Passion—The kind that makes you feel you're the object of desire.

The possibility of getting caught

Music

Moisture—A kiss that's a little on the wet side.

Darkness

The woman making the first move—Some men, however, do not like this.

Kissing foreplay—Or touching before actually kissing.

Caressing

Emotional involvement

Kissing Turnoffs

Bad breath—This is the number-one turnoff for everyone (see "Kissing Anxieties," page 106).

Wrong body position—One that feels awkward, uncomfortable, or inappropriate.

Slobbering

Long tongue

Facial hair stubble—Some women, however, like this.

Severe tongue sucking—Or sucking your partner's tongue with too much force.

Macho attitude

Eyes open

Leapfrogging—An illogical succession of kisses (kissing the forehead, moving to the kneecap, back up to the eyes, over the hand, and then down to the toes).

Starting a kiss with the mouth open too wide

Biting

Mechanical—Movements that lack emotion.

No participation from partner

Bad tongue movement—Especially movements that cause retching from your partner.

Kisses that are too wet

Lipstick—Since most adult men do not care for lipstick marks on their shirt or face.

Cold and/or sweaty hands

Too much lip pressure

Lifeless lips

Smoking

Tightly pursed lips—Prevent variation.

Something offensive in the mouth—Prior to the kiss (liver, gas siphon, chewing tobacco).

Earlier location of the hands—In dirt, touching diapers, in the nose.

Kissing the pet, then you

Picking teeth

False teeth

Too tentative

Not opening mouth—To receive a deep kiss.

Opening mouth too wide

Awkwardness

Tongue too far down the other's throat

Too much talking

Having eyelids kissed—If the receiver wears contacts or eye makeup.

Groping

Rushing—(Or failing to perform) the preliminaries.

Hands in the hair—Of a man who is going bald, or of a woman who has spent a lot of time putting it in place.

Kissing in public

Chapped lips

Dry, rough skin

Body odor

Look out for bad breath to strike . . .

- When you've been talking for an extended period of time.
- In the late afternoon. Saliva production drops when you haven't eaten or drunk for several hours.
- Before menstruation. Hormonal changes produce more sulfur compounds in the mouth.
- During exercise.
- When you have a cold.

Kissing Anxieties

NXIETY—it seems to be a part of our everyday life. Unfortunately, even the pleasurable act of kissing cannot escape this sensitivity. Kissing has its own set of anxiety issues: bad breath, mononucleosis, and AIDS.

Bad Breath

Officially, bad breath (or halitosis) is a foul breath odor emanating from the mouth, nose, or both. However you define it, bad breath is the number-one kissing turnoff by men and women alike. Halitosis has become a phobia with many because there's no absolute way of knowing whether or not your breath is offensive. Let's face it, no one short of your mother is going to tell you your breath could compete with a used cat litter box.

History has been harsh on the issue of bad breath. For example, an ancient Jewish law ordains that if a man marries a woman and finds out after the marriage that her breath is foul, not only can he divorce her, but also he is immediately exempt from any obligations that bind him in the marriage contract. Having bad breath can be a very serious problem.

Worry no more. You can now breathe easier. Here is the lowdown on the primary causes of bad breath and solutions for solving it.

CAUSES

Food Particles—Odor-producing bacteria live off the bits of food left in your mouth after eating. The longer the food debris sits, the more potent the stench.

Sulfur—Eating foods with a high sulfur content is a breath wrecker. When these foods are digested, the sulfur-containing compounds get into the bloodstream and eventually work their way into the lungs. In two to four hours the unpleasant smell referred to as "dog breath" appears. It can take up to twenty-four hours for it to clear out of your system and out of your breath.

Foods high in sulfur include: garlic, fish, horseradish, cabbage, onions, eggs, broccoli, Brussels sprouts, coffee, red meat, and red hot peppers. Cooking these foods, in some cases, can help reduce their effect on the breath. Also, eating parsley is said to help.

Pyrazine—This is another compound that can give a peculiar, though not necessarily bad, odor to the breath. It is found in nuts, coffee, chocolate, asparagus, green bell peppers, potato chips, and corn chips, bacon flavoring, and foods claiming a roasted flavor.

Alcohol—Beer, wine, and hard liquor have a distinctive aroma that gets into the bloodstream only to show up a few hours later as a fruity, unpleasant breath odor.

Some alcoholic beverages create a more potent breath odor than others because of the way they are made. Beer is brewed with hops, scotch is made with barley, and wine can be aged in oak barrels. All of these give the breath a stronger odor than, say, vodka, which is normally distilled from bland potatoes. Boozy breath can last up to twenty-four hours.

**BAD BREATH
SYNONYMS**

DINOSAUR BREATH
PASTA PERFUME
BRONX VANILLA
NOSE NUKER
DOG BREATH
ORDER OF FRIED ONIONS
GUTTER BREATH
SKUNK BREATH
HALITOSIS
TEARJERKER

Smoking—Cigarette, cigar, and pipe smoking guarantees bad breath. The smoke permeates not only the tissues of the mouth but also the hair, skin, and clothing. Smoker's breath can last up to seventy-two hours after smoking unless a thorough oral hygiene regimen is used shortly after smoking.

High-protein diet—Diets that include very little or no carbohydrates put the body in a state of ketosis, thereby giving the breath an unpleasant acetone scent. (This type of diet also makes for unpleasant body odor as well.)

Dehydration—Medications that dehydrate the body, such as antihistamines and motion-sickness pills, can cause foul-smelling breath. Certain diseases can also be the cause of "dry mouth." One solution is to drink fluids to rehydrate the body. Also, chewing sugarless gum or sucking on candy lemon drops can help stimulate the salivary glands and rehydrate the mouth.

Stress and exercise interrupt normal breathing and swallowing patterns, consequently reducing mouth moisture. If you notice a sour taste or a sticky feeling in your mouth, it should be a tip-off that your breath is uncertain. Again, chewing gum or eating something will help speed the rehydration process.

Sleep—"Morning breath" is simply dryness of the mouth. Saliva is a built-in breath freshener, continually cleaning and rinsing. However, when we sleep so do our salivary glands. (We swallow only twenty times during an average night's sleep versus two thousand times during the waking hours.) Snoring and open-mouthed breathing make the problem worse by further drying the mouth.

Morning breath is easily rectified by eating or drinking something to restimulate the salivary glands. A citrus juice is especially effective. Tartness jump-starts saliva flow into action.

Menstrual Cycle—Breath odor can occur for women around the time of ovulation. An increased level of estrogen triggers shedding of soft tissues throughout a woman's body, including mouth tissue, giving mouth bacteria more debris to feed on.

Gum Disease—Gum disease creates extremely offensive breath odor owing to the decomposing bacteria that collect in pockets around the teeth. A good oral hygiene program can eliminate the problem.

Stomach—Odors emanating from the contents of the stomach are extremely rare. The reason being the esophagus in our throat acts like a stopper to prevent any odors and gases from escaping. Belching and vomiting are usually the only times halitosis from the stomach will exist.

Health problems—Diabetes and kidney failure carry distinctive and very unpleasant breath odors. Ulcers or respiratory problems can also cause breath odor. In fact, foul breath can signal a nose, mouth, or throat infection. Any strong or unusual breath scent should be a tip-off to see a doctor.

SOLUTIONS

There are many causes of breath odor and no sure cure. Breath odor comes from both the mouth and the lungs, and the primary culprit, mouth bacteria, can't and shouldn't be completely removed due to their role in digestion. There are temporary solutions to the problem, however.

Gums, Mints, Drops, and Sprays—These are designed to mask breath odor, not fight or eliminate it. They do not remove trapped food particles, and only slightly stimulate saliva output. Some mints contain copper, which will temporarily neutralize the smell caused by sulfurous foods. Basically these products disguise foul breath for no more than ten to fifteen minutes, with drops and sprays lasting the longest because of their concentration.

Be sure these products are sugarless, because sugar requires digestion and therefore attracts more bacteria, as do the artificial sweeteners mannitol and sorbitol. The best breath sugar substitute reportedly is xylitol.

Mouthwashes—Mouthwashes are more effective because they swish away some food particles, kill some bacteria, mask some odors, and can last up to two hours. However, they are still only a temporary cure. Effective mouthwashes fall into two categories:

1. Those that neutralize sulfur smells with zinc chloride (mostly found in red mouthwashes).
2. Those that go after bacteria. Two ingredients to look for are domiphen bromide and cetylpyridinium chloride (usually found in yellow and green mouthwashes).

A recent discovery on the mouthwash front is oxidizing mouthwashes. Formulations which include chlorine dioxide have been shown to oxidize sulfur molecules, thus preventing them from entering the bloodstream. They work for up to eight hours.

Oral Hygiene—Brushing, flossing, and rinsing the mouth after eating is a winning program to combat bad breath. It is recommended that each brushing episode be five minutes, and that a toothbrush be put to pasture after three months if it is used three to four times a day. Flossing should be done once a day at bedtime and before brushing. Vigorous rinsing of your mouth,

Breath Freshening Tips:

- Brush and floss your teeth.
- Brush your tongue.
- Eat a low-fat, high-carbohydrate diet.
- Drink more water.

even with water, is a way to eliminate food particles and the bacteria that grow on them.

What most people don't realize is that the tongue needs to be brushed as well. A study by professor Joseph Tonzetich, Ph.D., in the School of Dentistry at the University of British Columbia in Vancouver, found that brushing the tongue is the single most effective method of decreasing breath odor. It is also recommended that the tissue inside the mouth be brushed since odor comes from the bacteria in the pockets of soft tissue that surround the teeth.

Increase Salivary Flow—Chewing or eating something fresh, raw, relatively bland tasting, and with a high water content will freshen your breath. Some foods to consider are apples, celery, carrots, watermelon, and oranges.

DETECTION
Here are three techniques that can be used to detect and locate the source of breath odor.

1. Lick the back of your hand or your wrist, wait a minute, then sniff. If odor-producing bacteria are at work in your mouth, there will be a decidedly sour odor.
2. Cup your hands, breathe out through the mouth, and then in through the nose. Normal breath has a slightly sweetish scent.

3. Find a good friend. Hold your breath and have the person sniff the inside of your mouth to see if it is the source of the odor. Next, breathe through your mouth. If the friend detects a bad odor, it's coming from the lungs. Finally, close your mouth and breathe through your nose. If your breath smells, you may have a sinus infection.

The good news about halitosis is that we worry about it more than we need to. One expert on oral hygiene products estimates that only one person in a hundred has noticeable bad breath without using a breath enhancer. Remember, too, that bad breath is in the nose of the beholder. It depends on what you're used to. But persistent, pernicious bad breath, of course, should be looked into by a dentist.

Kissing Disease

Thanks to Dr. Alfred S. Evans, infectious mononucleosis, or mono, has received the dubious nickname the "Kissing Disease." Evans coined the term while studying the Epstein-Barr virus (EBV) which is responsible for causing the illness.

Mono has traditionally been considered a badge of honor by teenagers since it is commonly transmitted through kissing. However, it is also known to be transmitted through close personal contact as well. It is most common among young people between the ages of fifteen and twenty-five where they are in proximity to others their age, such as in college dorms.

Saliva exchange through kissing is the primary, but not the exclusive, method for transmission of mono. Coughing or sneezing can cause small droplets of infected saliva and/or mucus to be suspended in the air, which can be inhaled by others and cause the disease. Sharing food or beverages from the same container or utensil can also transfer the virus from one person to another. Once the virus has infected an individual, a period of four to eight weeks generally passes before that person becomes ill.

The initial symptoms of mono are a general lack of energy or malaise, a loss of appetite, and chills. These initial symptoms can last from one to three days before the more intense symptoms of the illness begin.

The next stage of mono is marked by a fever from 102 to 104 degrees, a very reddened throat and tonsils, and swollen lymph glands in the neck.

Mono has no known cure. Therefore, no specific treatment is warranted. For the most part, providing supportive and comforting measures and allowing the person to receive sufficient amounts of rest and sleep are all that is necessary. Of course, the best cure is not to kiss someone who is infected.

AIDS

To date, there are absolutely no known cases of people contracting AIDS from French kissing. According to the AIDS hotline (800-342-AIDS), traces of the AIDS virus have been found in saliva, but the concentrations are believed to be too small to cause infection. However, getting AIDS from French kissing is considered "theoretically possible" if the person infected with the AIDS virus has blood in his mouth, and it is mingled with a cut in his partner's mouth. Again, there are no known cases being spread this way, but if you want to play it safe, get to know your kissing partner before you kiss him or her.

Lipstick Personality

Did you know the shape of your lipstick says alot about your personality? Well, find out what your lipstick reveals about you and could reveal about others.

- **Flat Top:** Levelheaded, self-assured, high morals, dependable, loves a challenge.
- **Wedge:** Loyal, won't gossip, likes attention, opinionated, dislikes schedules.
- **Valley:** Inquisitive, researches, makes friends easily, adventurous, complex, exciting.
- **Rounded:** Friendly, generous, flirty, easygoing, even-tempered, peacemaker, likable.
- **Steeple:** Sensual, daring, stubborn, domestic, a "doer," family-oriented, exaggerates.
- **Original Shape:** Follows rules, self-conscious, somewhat reserved, likes schedules.

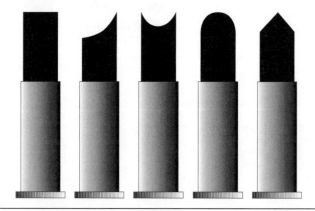

Kissing as an Art Form

Advice from the Experts

HAT DO THE PROS have to say about kissing? Well, you're about to find out. Over one hundred kissing experts were asked a series of questions, and their answers make up this chapter.

Before starting, however, let's explain who these kissing experts are. Since most people, when asked, claim to be good kissers, the challenge was to find the truly noteworthy. Therefore, the experts were those who were referrals by others as being exceptional kissers.

To See or Not to See

Studies on eye position while kissing have discovered that most women keep them closed, and more than 30 percent of men keep them open. Almost all of our experts kiss with their eyes closed. Only a handful of men claimed to keep their eyes opened. Many commented, however, that they will occasionally open their eyes during a kiss to see how their partner is doing.

Advocates of closed eyes claim "It sets a better mood" and "It allows for more imagination." Moreover, "You have no distractions so you can concentrate on what you're doing." "It just feels sexier."

As for those who straddle the fence, they say, "Close your eyes when you're kissing on the lips because you're too close to focus. Otherwise, open your eyes so you can hit what you're aiming at." They also made the point that you need not close your eyes for a social or friendly kiss, though it's appropriate to do so for intimacy.

Our handful of open-eyed kissers insisted that it's more sensual and more intense. On a practical note, they like to see the effect they're having on their partner.

To Beard or Not to Beard

Most women don't like to kiss men with facial hair for reasons of cleanliness and discomfort—"It hurts!" Most men have heard, and sympathize with their complaints. The fashion of men wearing three-day-old stubble met with mixed reviews. If the stubble was soft, most felt it was O.K. Mustaches had a higher tolerance level than beards.

On Lipstick Traces

For the most part, men do not like lipstick, claiming, "It's for decoration only; it does nothing to enhance the kiss." It does, however, increase dry cleaning bills, they complained. "If it's very light, then it's all right," said some, while others agreed that

"Painted lips are great to look at; clean, fresh lips are preferred for kissing."

Most women advise: "Wear lipstick to attract him, but then don't wear it when you decide you want him to kiss you." One woman even suffered the embarrassment of having a man offer her a handkerchief to remove her lipstick. Of course, "Just the right amount, worn properly, can invite a kiss."

A Kiss is Just a Kiss,
but Some Kisses are Better Than Others

Here's what the experts had to say about their most memorable kisses:

"My first kiss was the first time I ever experienced that nervous, excited feeling that goes down from your lips, pushing your stomach onto the floor."

"We 'made eyes' at each other for a while, then had a long, slow-motion start. Our mouths barely opened, and our tongues just barely touched."

"Once, I was truly taken by surprise. I experienced the most powerful kiss; I was really shaken up for about an hour. I can't even describe it—you had to be there."

"He started very slowly and softly, and miraculously knew just when and how to build up the tempo and the passion until he literally left me breathless."

"My best kiss was with a twenty-one-year-old blonde who was convinced she would go to hell for kissing a married man but wanted to anyway."

"It happened in the middle of a conversation. We'd kiss. We'd talk. We'd kiss some more, then talk some more. Eventually, we were just kissing."

"My best kisses have always come after my best margaritas."

"When I was in the seventh grade, I experienced my first 'French kiss'—with an older woman. (She was thirteen.) I think it was nerves, or the anticipation, or the thrill of doing something for the first time. I still think about it twenty years later."

"I was in my father's car, and I left the motor running while we kissed good-night. I went through half a tank of gas."

Memorable Kisses You'd Rather Forget

Both men and women vividly recall "limp and lifeless tongues," and being slobbered on by people who had large mouths or too much to drink. One woman even claims to have had her waterproof mascara licked off. Then, of course, there's stubble burn, bad breath, too much pressure, and body odor.

Men spoke of times when they were young and inexperienced—before they knew what went where. One had even been laughed at (and it wasn't his fault). Nobody likes kissing without participation from his or her partner.

How Do You Like to Be Held?

"I don't," responded one gentleman. "I like to focus on the kiss and minimize other sensations."

Men like to be held gently, and they enjoy having fingers run through their hair. Women, on the other hand, like to be held firmly—not too firmly, though—and do not like hands running through their hair if it has been "fixed." They also don't like hands on their face if they are wearing makeup and don't like hands landing on inappropriate body parts. Everyone likes to be caressed, and lying down together was the most mentioned kissing position while being held.

What Are Your Tricks of the Trade?

When asked what makes them good kissers, the experts responded: spontaneity, natural ability, tenderness, sensitivity, and passion. Several also mentioned kissing while they are themselves (rather than drunk or high). Some were taught by great kissers, and their partners thoroughly enjoy it—and it shows. One man said simply, "I'm French. Need I say more?"

When is the Time Right?

People are pretty ambiguous about timing. Most suggested, "You can see it in their eyes," "You can feel it," or "The mood is right." All preferred to kiss while sober, claiming they could experience feelings more fully and kissing seemed to provide its own high. One suggested, "Kiss as though you have all the time in the world, but don't prolong a kiss beyond its natural life." Others recommended, "Just kiss when you can't wait any longer."

Can You Tell Before You Kiss Someone?

The experts were asked if they could tell whether or not someone would be a good kisser (before kissing). Not one expert could state for certain that a future kissing partner would be a good kisser before actually kissing them. It just goes to show, you can't judge a kisser by the cover.

When Isn't a Kiss Romantic?

When asked to describe their funniest or most awkward kiss, the respondents had some colorful stories:

"I opened my eyes to see if his were closed. To my horror, he was just staring at me."

"We sent for something to eat after barhopping all evening. When he bent down to kiss me, he forgot to take

his toothpick out of his mouth. Needless to say, I got poked."

"I got a nosebleed in the middle of a very passionate kiss."

"All I can say is, don't burp."

"We were kissing, passionately, and I happened to have been standing on a mound of dirt (so I could reach him). I slipped, and he opened his eyes to find me staring at his zipper."

"The slats on the bed broke. We fell to the floor, and woke everyone up with a crash."

"We were kissing, and my dog surprised my date by biting his crotch."

"On our first date, he started leaning in to kiss me but I dropped my purse. We ended up knocking heads, with him having a huge knot on his forehead."

"Once, when I was in high school, I went parking. My car sank into the mud during the two hours we kissed. I had to get it towed out."

"As a bubble gum-chewing teenager, I kissed a girl with braces. It all happened so fast, but we were stuck together for quite some time."

"I used to have a tooth in the roof of my mouth. (I've since had a root canal to remove it.) A girl discovered it with her tongue. She leapt back, turned white, and asked

me what it was. I told her it was gum, and refused to kiss her anymore."

Some Pointers From the Pros

The experts were asked to share their special techniques:

"Slip your arms around the nape of his neck or around his waist. Snuggle close to him. Then close your eyes and touch your lips to his. Try not to stiffen your lips—keep them soft and relaxed. Give yourself time to warm up. Start with gentle kisses, then let feelings gradually build."

"Softer is better and gentle is best. Technique is important, but what matters most is the connection that grows between two people after the lips have met."

"Passion is at the heart of how we imagine a really great kiss."

"When it comes to hands, use them but in nonerotic zones. Graze gently. Good spots are the back, shoulders, and arms. Some like it on their behinds."

"Gently run your tongue across the person's eyelids, and then across the brows, or lick your partner's lips."

To show that he's taken your breath away, one woman advises *"pull away, catch your breath, and lightly moan after a kiss."*

"Move to a rhythm—the rhythm is in your head; you don't have to hear it."

"Generally speaking, relax, be creative, be tender, take your time, and work your way up to a passionate kiss. It goes without saying that you should really care for the person you're kissing."

"As soon as you finish a kiss, lightly blow into your partner's mouth."

"If your partner is good at kissing—say so. People like to hear it."

"A loving kiss should bestow an intoxicating feeling of infinite happiness."

Extraordinary Kissing

THE SCUTTLEBUTT about musicians who play woodwind or brass instruments is that they are the best kissers because their lip muscles are highly developed. Though this speculation merits some consideration, don't go out and sign up for tuba lessons just yet. There is more to being an outstanding kisser than just great lip muscle tone.

Being extraordinary means going beyond what is usual, customary, or required. Many musicians can perform with technical competency, yet what leads one to outperform another is his or her ability to go beyond mere proficiency.

Emotional involvement, sensitivity, and a respect for the music and the instrument set the stars apart. Great kissing requires more than blueprint accuracy. There are essentially six qualities that go into extraordinary kissing.

Imagination

What gives kissing surprise, excitement, and intrigue is imagination. Everyone has the ability to be imaginative; if you think you're not, you're wrong. Think about how you fill out your income tax form, embellish your fishing stories, and organize your clothes. All that took some kind of imagination. Part of being imaginative is the ability to be resourceful. The next time you watch television, read a romantic novel, or go to the movies, study how the kisses are enacted. Then be open to using those ideas during your next kiss.

Try creating kisses that belong exclusively to you and your partner. Kiss your partner so he or she responds with an "ooh," and "aah," and a quickened pulse. Develop a way to send kisses through the telephone. A distinctive kiss not only shows imagination but sends your partner the signal that he or she is special.

Experimentation

Observing, understanding, and then being able to enhance the qualities that give your partner the greatest pleasure is what extraordinary kissing is all about. Experimenting with different kinds of kisses helps you find those qualities in your partner.

Try for example using different embraces, kissing places other than the lips, or varying the intensity of your kisses. While doing this, pay attention to your partner's responses. You'll soon discover his or her preferences.

Kissing games such as spin the bottle, post office, name that kiss, bobbing for tongues, and king of the mouth provide a great medium for experimentation. Send messages to your partner in kissing Morse code, or tongue wrestle.

Kissing games can also center around food. Have a food fight between mouths. Or try sharing something like licorice, starting at the same time but at opposite ends. Have you ever played mouth hockey? Start with an M&M held between the tips of your tongues. The goal is the back of your partner's mouth. The game begins after the third nose rub and ends when either the M&M dissolves or one of you eats it.

Kissing experimentation ought to be an ongoing practice. With a little creativity, your kisses never will be boring.

Kindness

Kissing with kindness is like eating with table manners. It is easier to be kissed by a person who shows kindness than someone who tries to slam-dunk you onto a couch before learning your name.

The Golden Rule seems to have been all but forgotten these days. However, it is a great rule in kissing. If you "do unto others as you would have others do unto you" during a kiss, you will help the person you're with feel more comfortable. You also show your partner by example how you want to be treated. Take this quick kindness quiz:

1. Have you made sure your partner is comfortable before beginning to kiss?
2. Is your partner relaxed (not just drunk)?
3. Do you make an effort to detect what kind of kissing your partner likes?
4. Would you like to be kissed the way you're kissing your partner?
5. If asked, would your partner say you are tender and gentle?

If you answered no to any of these questions, you haven't been entirely kind.

When the two of you operate on the same "kindness wavelength," your kissing naturally becomes extraordinary. Also know that kindness should be mutual. If you're not receiving kindness in return for yours, you need to rethink the person and the situation.

Confidence

Confident kissing carries the conviction that no matter what happens, you can manage any kissing situation. If your first

attempt at a kiss doesn't work, you don't retreat into a hole
and declare your lips sacred virginal ground. You regroup and
try a different approach. Confident kissing means you have
faith in your kissing skills.

If you've had poor aim, suffered criticism, or been desert-
ed in the past, learn from your mistakes and then declare
them history. Future partners will know nothing about your
past kissing traumas. It's one of the few opportunities in life
where you get a fresh start.

Recognize that confident kissing takes
time to develop. First you must overcome
kissing worries: How far will it go? How will
your partner react: Laugh? Pant? Yawn? How
will you perform? If or when should you use
your tongue? Is your breath okay? Remember
that there's no one magical, surefire way to
kiss anyone. The two of you are in the same
boat: neither has kissed the other before. Like
running on a treadmill, worrying gets you all
worked up, but it doesn't get you anywhere.

Kissing Games

Kiss the Pillow
A game played by
adolescent girls either
alone or with their
friends. They pretend
their pillow is a kissing
partner and practice lip
movements and
embraces.

Also realize that no one's clocking how
long you take getting to first base. And a kiss does not have to
take place before concluding the first date, or the second, or
the third. Take your time and become familiar with the other
person. Don't think about all the things that might go wrong.
Instead, look forward to the future kiss you are contemplating.

It helps to do a little research. Discover your date's
favorite music, sports, his or her alma mater. Familiarity

strengthens confidence. A final point on confidence: remember that the line between self-confidence and conceit is a fine one. Be open to the possibility that your kissing can always stand improvement.

Communication

That our lips are designed to form kisses, as well as words, gives proof positive that the two should always go hand-in-hand.

Without conversation, a kiss can be misconstrued. Suppose your partner kisses you ambiguously during a first date, then goes forward with a conversation on something completely unrelated. There are now several questions running through your mind. Was the kiss done out of obligation or affection? Or was it merely an experiment? And if so, how did you rate? You will probably spend a good deal of time running the scenario by your best friends for their interpretation. Such needless wondering can be eliminated by communicating.

HICKEY KISSONYMS

HOOVER
STRAWBERRY KISS
KISS BITE
VAC ATTACK
MONKEY BITE

Conversing with your partner also uncovers your partner's kissing preferences. Even one word ("Wow") after a kiss announces your partner's enthusiasm. Dialogue on other topics helps you gain insights into your partner, which help you feel more comfortable and perhaps less vulnerable. Conversation makes each kiss better than the one before.

You can also communicate with your partner through notes, cards, letters, the Internet, a video, a poem, or a riddle. Or get your message across with some unusual communication means like charades, a Pictionary game, a palm reader (with a previously well-greased palm), an impersonator, Western Union, or even David Letterman's viewer mail. Sharing more thoughts with your partner can only make the kisses between you better. Howl like dogs if you want; just communicate.

Good communication is as stimulating as black coffee and just as hard to sleep after. The same can be said of a good kiss. Enjoy communicating and kissing and worry about sleeping later.

Respect

Respecting the person you kiss means you find that person valuable and worthy of special treatment. Mutual respect neutralizes many of our unattractive tendencies and forces our motives to be honorable. When you respect someone, you show your best side; you want to please, and you pay attention.

You may be showing a lack of respect for your partner without realizing it. Ask yourself these questions:

1. Have you ever kissed someone you didn't care for?
2. Have you ever kissed to get something you wanted?
3. Have you ever kissed just to make another person jealous?

4. Have you ever used a kiss to lead someone on?
5. Have you ever used a kiss as a weapon?
6. Have you ever kissed someone out of guilt or obligation?

A "yes" to any one of these questions shows you weren't respecting your partner. If you don't care for someone, don't kiss them. By refusing to kiss indiscriminately, you increase the value of your kisses.

You may be showing respect, but not getting it in return. Put yourself in your partner's shoes and see if you're stepping on toes. Pay attention to timing. A kiss shortly after a first meeting is a red flag; holding off gives time for you to develop regard and admiration for each other.

A shocking fact to many is that most extraordinary kissers today are over the age of fifty. The explanation is really quite simple: They kissed during courting. This generation understood that kissing was an important phase of courtship, and they clocked more hours doing it than today's younger generation. Kissing stood on its own and many times was the only shared intimacy between two people until they married.

The lesson to be learned by this fact is to take things slowly, one step at a time. Don't skip hand-holding and hugging. A kiss is best when shared with someone you really like. When that kiss finally happens it will no doubt be fabulous. And if you're in love with the person, it will be out of this world.

Now that you know what it takes to be extraordinary, go for it! Kiss with imagination, experimentation, kindness, confidence, communication, and respect, and outstanding results are almost guaranteed.

Kissing Socially

"I'm not kissing anybody on the cheek anymore.
I hate that."

STEVE MARTIN

in *L.A. Story*

♥

SOCIAL KISSING in America has become a system of chaos and uncertainty. If you go to Paris, you know you'll get the ritual three-cheek kiss, so you are prepared and can get into the rhythm. We, however, have too many variations, and our social kissing is plagued with surprise.

Equally concerning is the fact that we don't feel safe from the unsolicited social kiss. It's showing up everywhere. Friendly gatherings, business functions, and, of course, parties have turned into battlegrounds laced with lip land mines that go off without warning. Even when it's acceptable to kiss socially, we're not sure which kiss to perform.

To make some sense out of all of this lip service, it is best to segment social kissing into two categories: sociable kissing and business kissing. Sociable kissing occurs when you bump into a friend or are attending a gathering of personal friends and acquaintances. Business kissing includes kissing at business functions or at gatherings with current or potential business associates.

Sociable Kissing

Sociable kissing as a greeting has become very commonplace these days, and that's really a pity. Many of us feel these sociable kisses are meaningless, phony, or insincere. In addition to distrust, we feel confused and frustrated because unlike a handshake, these kisses never seem to go smoothly; while you aim for their cheek, they may be aiming for a direct hit on the lips.

A basic rule in sociable kissing is to only kiss someone at a social gathering because you consider them very special—too good for a handshake or a nod. Don't kiss indiscriminately.

Often, more than one of your dearest friends will attend the same party. Do you kiss them all and risk being branded an insincere kisser? Well, another rule or guideline is to not kiss more than six people. If you are kissing more, you should stop and ask yourself what you're doing. Either you're everyone's best friend, or you're not being selective enough, thereby devaluing your kisses. It's smarter to err on the side of kissing too few people. Just remember that handshakes and hugs are gestures of greeting as well.

Here are a few more guidelines to help you muddle through those social gatherings:

1. Between the two of you, the one deemed "more important" (ranking family member, host, honored guest) has the right to initiate the kiss. If this distinction isn't obvious, then the woman gets the right by default.

2. The woman chooses what to offer up for the kiss (lips, a cheek, or a hand); the man must oblige with one exception. If she offers her hand, the man has the option of either kissing or shaking it.

3. There is no penalty for not kissing.

4. If someone takes you by surprise with a kiss, don't show your annoyance or disgust. The person was wrong, but the whole incident will soon be forgotten.

Some social situations, in addition to friendly gatherings, automatically come with a sociable kissing permit. For example, when:

• You greet your spouse.
• Someone you like receives an honor or recognition.
• You hear news that calls for congratulations.
• Considerable time has passed since you've seen or spoken to the person.
• You greet family and friends at celebrations or holidays.
• Attending occasions of sadness or suffering, to show your sympathy and affection.

- Receiving a gift.
- Leaving for or returning from an adventure (lengthy trip, camp, boarding school, college, military service).

Once you've determined that a sociable kiss is appropriate, you are now left with the dubious task of determining which sociable kiss to perform. Though our list is not complete, here are some options for you to consider:

Sociable Kisses

Classic cheek—A kiss used as a gesture of greeting. An alternative to a handshake.

Air smack—Approaching as if to kiss the cheek of the other but instead making a noisy kiss in the open air near the cheek. The cheeks come very close but do not touch.

Double air smack—An air smack on each side.

Socially conservative smack—While shaking right hands with your partner, lean forward, twisting your mouth as far to the left as possible, and lightly touch right jaws.

Sideswipe smack—With the two of you standing side-by-side, brush the inside cheek while puckering your lips. (Sound is optional.)

Over-the-shoulder kiss—Performed for the benefit of seeing who's behind the kissee, it is the gesture of the air smack without the noise. Also called "a mingling of perfumes."

The hummingbird—With the mouth firmly closed, the kisser lightly touches the partner's cheek with his or her own while invoking a humming sound.

Goldfish kiss—Also called the cheek-to-cheek kiss. With both parties holding their lips in a tight pucker, each brushes the cheek of the other without making a sound or spoiling any lipstick. A popular social kiss among women.

Social French kiss—A kiss commonly implemented by French officials. Grasping the upper arms of the other, place a pressure kiss on each cheek. Begin with the right cheek and then swing to the left one. Make sure the noses do not collide.

French-to-French—A social kiss with both parties participating in the kissing of the other's cheek. The two parties may perform this kiss either simultaneously, or one can wait until the other is finished before beginning the kiss.

Group kiss—This kiss is used to acknowledge a group of people affectionately. The people closest to you receive air smacks or goldfish kisses. The people too far away to reach are blown kisses.

Kiss the hand—Man to woman. The man pretends to kiss the top side of the woman's hand, but his lips never actually touch.

Two-handed lean—Walking forward with both hands outstretched, grab the two hands of your partner and form a circle. Each then leans into the circle and kisses the other on the lips or brushes the cheeks.

Kissing Games

Name that Kiss

Your partner engages you in a variety of kisses, and you must name it correctly or be forced to endure the same kiss again until you get the name right. You then switch places.

Sociable kissing may be on the rise, but that doesn't mean you have to participate. Kissing is a very powerful gesture. Use it honestly and selectively. Also, make a mental note of how people feel about receiving your sociable kisses. Next time, you will be better able to act more appropriately and comfortably.

Four techniques for fending off unwanted, oncoming kissers:

1. Quickly move forward and grasp the person's upper right arm (near the shoulder) with your left hand to neutralize the person. Then, grasp the right hand with yours in a warm handshake. The initiator is forced to comply.

2. Offer your hand while keeping your arm rigid. If the person tries to come at you for a kiss, use your hand-clasp as leverage to hold the person "off." If you're overpowered, give in, but turn a very "cold cheek."

3. Take the person's hand in yours and cup it with your other hand. This gesture shows your warmth and that you like the person; at the same time it lets you escape the kiss.

4. Unexpectedly bend down and begin tying your shoe.

Business Kissing

Extending a hand used to be the only acceptable greeting in business. Now business kissing is making its mark in the business world. This phenomenon is on the increase, and in many cases it is replacing the handshake.

This increase in business puckering grew out of two trends: a continued blurring of the distinction between social and business etiquette and an increase of women in the workplace.

Kisses planted on corporate cheeks have caused a potential land mine in corporate America because one misjudged action can cost corporate points. There is definitely a pecking order with kissing in the workplace.

As with sociable kissing, there are varying opinions on business kissing. Some believe it's a social blunder unless the kissers are close friends outside the workplace. Others believe that kissing obscures the line and rank of command in a company, which lessens professionalism and credibility. Some even suggest it negatively accentuates gender differences. Sealing a business deal with a kiss has no legal grounds, and many compare it to giving to charity: Once you start, you'll be expected to give every time you meet.

There are potentially two issues in business kissing: whether or not it's appropriate; and if so, how it should be executed. Before putting your lips into action there are some variables to be considered:

Business Kissing Variables

City	Location
Age	Onlookers
Rank	Personal Relationship
Gender	Previous Relationship
Occasion	

You must also take into account the industry in which you work, since every industry has its own culture.

Kiss Happy Industries

Film/Media	Hotel and Restaurant
Fine Arts	Modeling
Advertising	Cosmetics
Apparel	Public Relations

Non-Kissing Industries

Banking	Medicine
Engineering	Health Care
Law	Government
Manufacturing	Distribution
Accounting	Insurance
Data Processing	Fast Food

When the occasion arises, be armed and prepared. Here are the basics of business kissing to help you through this difficult and often awkward gesture:

Do:

- Kiss in a business situation if you know the person well.
- Kiss at business parties and other social functions.
- Only touch cheeks or kiss the air.
- Let your superior be the one to initiate the kiss.
- Use a handshake if it will equally satisfy the situation.

Don't:

- Kiss strangers or upon meeting someone for the first time.
- Leave a lipstick mark on the person being kissed.
- Kiss in strictly business environments such as the office or conference room.

- Play favorites and kiss only those you like best. Be consistent with your selection.
- Let people kiss you if you don't feel comfortable about it.
- Kiss directly on the lips.
- Kiss if either party has had alcohol. Sobriety is a must.

If you're still not sure, it's safer not to risk a business kiss. And for those business associates who you believe are worthy of more than the traditional handshake, there are alternative greetings that offer warmth without requiring that you take or give any lip:

The Half Hug—Shake right hands while you each put your left hand on the other's right upper arm or shoulder. This "almost" hug is acceptable in the office.

The Hand Cup Shake—Join right hands and cup the handshake with your left hand.

The Hug and Pat—A very loose hug leaves light between the two of you while you pat the other on the back.

The Back Pat—Approach the person from his or her left side and pat the person on the back with your right hand. A handshake may immediately follow.

Kiss Avoidance Lines:

- "I'd like to kiss you, but I just washed my hair."
- "My lips are too sunburned."
- "I'm suddenly coming down with something."
- "I tend to bite my partner's lips off."
- "I just ate liver."
- "If you kiss me, I'll have to kill you."
- "I'm afraid you'll think I'm easy if I let you."
- "Your kiss might bother my nose job."
- "I have to get permission from my minister."

Business kissing has the potential for abuse in the business world when it can be exploited to someone's advantage.

"Power Kissers" use kissing to leverage a better business position for themselves.

A power kiss is affectionless, but it makes some sort of power play. Recipients of power kisses should be aware that the gesture can be considered a put-down. A man might kiss a female business peer simply to send the message to others that he's the one who's really in charge. A woman who conspicuously offers up a cheek demanding an adoring peck, yet does not reciprocate, insinuates that the man is beneath her. Power kissing, if misconstrued, can become the makings of hot office gossip.

The victim of a power kiss can discourage future attempts by initiating the kiss and planting it on the cheek or by avoiding the kiss altogether, intercepting it with a handshake.

Business kissing is an acceptable greeting in certain industries and situations, but be aware that you always take on some risk when you initiate even a harmless business kiss. Here are some final points:

- Don't kiss someone you don't know well. The longer you've known someone, the more appropriate a friendly peck will be.
- Consider the occasion and setting. Kissing exchanges during social business gatherings such as banquets, conventions, and office parties may be acceptable. However, it's bad form in strictly business settings, e.g. the office, conference rooms, board meetings.
- Avoid kissing superiors and subordinates. Junior-level personnel pecking upper-level management or their

spouses may be interpreted as trying to gain favor. Kissing down the ranks can get you in trouble, too, if it's interpreted as inappropriate advances or harassment from someone who is abusing his or her power.

- Don't let yourself be kissed unless you want to. Avoid kisses by being quick on the draw with a handshake.
- Don't worry if your kiss is not reciprocated. The person may have been caught off guard. However, make a mental note of that person's behavior so you will know next time.
- Don't worry about misses. If you go for the cheek and end up on the lips or in their hair, just keep on trucking and laugh it off.

Kissing Embraces

KISSING, by design, arouses a natural desire for more body contact with your partner, and fortunately, there are many ways to arrange your body in order to make this happen. Here is a list of various kissing embraces to try. In an effort to keep these descriptions simple and succinct, the partner who should be either taller, stronger, heavier, or the primary initiator in each embrace is cast as the man. (Feel free to reverse roles.)

With Both Standing

Basic front-to-front embrace—This is the most common kissing embrace. Standing in front of his partner, he places his hands on her waist. She places her hands on his waist and tilts her head backward. Hands may hold shoulders, neck, or even the face as a variation.

Kissing Games

Mouth Hockey

Start with an M&M candy held between the tips of your tongues. The goal is the back of your partner's mouth. The game begins after the third nose rub and ends when either the M&M dissolves or one of you eats it.

Sandwich embrace—She stands with her back to a wall. He, standing in front, places his hands on the wall, in a playful, nonthreatening "gotcha" manner.

Bearhug embrace—With his feet on each side of hers, he locks his arms around her upper torso to hold her tightly. She wraps her arms around his waist.

Steam press embrace—He wraps his arms around her upper back and applies light pressure to keep the two bodies close together. Her arms are at her side or around his neck. It is popular for the man to lift the woman off her feet.

Hook embrace—She passes her hands under his arms and then reaches up to grab the back of his shoulders. He wraps his arms around her waist.

Chaste embrace—Standing approximately twelve inches apart, holding hands, both lean forward to kiss.

Dancer embrace—Standing face-to-face, he holds her right hand in his left and encircles her waist with his right arm. She rests her left hand on his right shoulder.

Dirty dancer embrace—Same body position as the "Dancer," except her left hand and his right hand relocate to the other's derrière.

Dirtier dancer embrace—Both hands of each partner rest on both cheeks of their partner's derrière.

Hanger embrace—With her body and face tilted considerably backward, she wraps her arms around his neck and lightly hangs while he holds on to her upper arms. This embrace will feel awkward unless the man is noticeably taller than the woman.

Front-to-Back Embraces

Basic front-to-back embrace—He stands behind her and wraps his arms around her waist. This is a popular embrace for surprising or distracting your partner. It is also used by couples when waiting in line.

The following three embraces are variations on this stance.

- **Necktie embrace**—She arches backward and stretches her arms above and slightly behind her head and wraps them around his neck.
- **Cradle embrace**—She leans backward, rests her head on his shoulder, and reaches back to put her hands in his rear pants pockets.

- **Sidewinder embrace**—She stands behind him with her hands on his waist. She then leans to one side, nudges her head under his arm, and then up to his face for a kiss.

With One Standing, the Other Sitting

Note: The impact of the following embraces will vary with the choice of sitting object (chair, stool, counter, bed).

Front-to-Front Embraces

- **Wrapper embrace**—The seated woman wraps her legs around the legs of her standing partner, encircles his waist with her arms, and tilts her head back.
- **Corner pocket embrace**—He sits with his legs parted. She stands between his legs and holds onto him around his neck. He holds onto her waist.
- **Cage embrace**—The standing man leans forward and places his hands on the arms of her chair. She, keeping her hands in her lap, tilts her head back to receive the kiss.

Front-to-Back Embraces

- **Bend and stretch embrace**—The seated woman stretches her head back, while the man behind bends forward. His hands rest on her shoulders.
- **Harness embrace**—He leans over the seated woman and wraps his arms loosely around her neck.
- **Rubdown embrace**—Standing behind her, he runs his hands down the woman's arms and leans forward to give

her a kiss. She reaches back with her hands to run them down his legs.

Sitting on the Other's Lap

- **Basic lap embrace**—Sitting with her legs across his lap, she wraps her arms around his neck. His arms rest around her waist. She may also hold his hand.
- **Lap cradle**—She sits on his left knee and leans into his left shoulder. His left hand is placed around her shoulders, his right hand on her cheek.
- **Lap stack embrace**—Sitting on his lap as if it were a chair, she leans backward and lays her head on one of his shoulders. His arms come forward to wrap around her waist. There are two variations on this:
  1. His arms rest around her shoulders, and her hands come up to rest on his arms.
  2. He places his hands on her legs, and she places her hands on top of his hands.
- **Lap straddle embrace**—Straddling his lap, she wraps her arms around his neck. He holds on to her by wrapping his arms around her waist.

Couch Embraces

Basic couch potato embrace—He reclines with the back of his head in her lap. She, seated, rests one arm on his chest, the other arm at her side, under his head, or holding his free hand.

Back-against-the-couch embrace—Sitting on the floor with his back resting against the couch, he parts and bends his legs. She sits between his legs and leans back against his chest. Her hands rest on the top of his bent legs. His arms encircle her waist.

Sports potato embrace—Any embrace that allows him to kiss while keeping one eye on the score. One arm must always be free to express "high five" gestures or to operate the remote control.

Couch à la carte embrace—Any couch embrace that enables one partner to reach the food on the coffee table.

Anti-voyeur embrace—Any couch embrace that hides the two of you from nearby siblings, roommates, or parents.

With Both Reclining

Basic stack embrace—She, lying face down on top of him, puts her hands under his head or shoulders. He wraps his arms around her body. (This is a good position when kissing is going to last a while.)

Roller embrace—Basic stack embrace with the partners taking turns on top by rolling to one side.

Basic reclining-on-your-side embrace—Both lie on their side and face one another. Her other arm wraps around his shoulders. His closest arm to the ground goes just under her arm. His top arm wraps around her waist. Designed to have as much body surface touching the other as possible. (Warning: Arms may fall asleep if not in the proper locations.)

Frog embrace—Woman on top has her legs in the frog position.

Spread-eagle embrace—He lies on the floor face up with his arms spread and legs slightly parted. She lies on top of the man face down and mirrors his position.

Catamaran embrace—Both lying face down, each partner's head turns toward the other. Closest arm around the other. (Also called the kissamaran.)

Embraces for Every Occasion

Threshold embrace—He holds her in his arms as if she were his bride and carries her across the threshold.

Yin and Yang embrace—Each lies on his or her side in a semi-fetal position. The two hook together at the lips from opposite directions.

Bridge embrace—Both lying head-to-head on their stomachs on the floor, each arches up on his or her elbows and holds the other's hands.

Casanova embrace—Standing profile to her partner, she leans back onto his outstretched left arm. While she holds on to his lower right arm, he further tilts back her face with his right hand to plant a kiss on her upturned lips.

Carousel embrace—With the two of you in a standing embrace, rotate clockwise or counterclockwise as you kiss. Some like to simulate a carousel and bob up and down as they circle.

Twirl embrace—She grasps his neck with her arms. He takes her by the waist and lifts her off her feet. He then twirls around in a circle and the two exchange a long kiss.

"Gotcha" embrace—The woman lies on her back with her hands above her head. The man sits on her waist and playfully holds her wrists with his hands as if to pin her down.

Basic buddy embrace—Standing shoulder-to-shoulder, you encircle your partner with the arm closest to his or her waist. Popular for walking together. Other hand positions are on necks or shoulders.

Kayak embrace—The woman sits behind her partner with her legs outside of his. The upper part of her body leans forward to be in close contact with his back. She wraps her arms tightly around his waist. Kisses are places principally along the back of his neck and the sides of his face. Variations on this embrace include:

1. She pokes her head under one of his arms to be kissed on the face.

2. She wraps her legs around his waist, and her arms encircle his chest.

3. He leans his head back to rest on one of her shoulders, making it possible for her to kiss his cheek and mouth.

A Listing of Kisses

VEN IF IT WERE your favorite food, you would grow tired of it if it were served to you over and over again. You'd soon welcome a change. Likewise, the same holds true for kissing. The same kiss again and again can become tedious and mechanical.

Here is relief for anyone's kissing rut. The following is a collection of kisses. They are the product of research, experience, and a little ingenuity.

Simple Kisses

Simple kiss—A lip-to-lip kiss with both parties applying light pressure.

Kisslet—A kiss where the lips barely touch.

Pressure kiss—A kiss with notable lip pressure.

Peck—A quick pressure kiss that concludes with a smacking lip sound.

Prolonged kiss—A kiss sustained longer than is considered normal. The pressure during this kiss alternates between light and heavy.

Corner kiss—Kissing the corners of the mouth, one at a time.

Pressed kiss—A simple kiss with your partner's lower lip pressed between your two lips.

Greatly pressed kiss—Holding your partner's lower lip between your two fingers, touch it with your tongue. Then replace your fingers with your lips and press his or her lower lip with force.

Pouting kiss—A kiss with your lips pouting.

Kiss of innocence—Standing a few feet apart and facing one another, the woman places her hands in his. Both close their eyes and lean forward until lips meet in a kiss.

Knob kiss—A kiss with lips over-puckered.

Fish kiss—A kiss with "fish lips." (Separate your teeth and suck in your cheeks until the corners of your mouth meet.)

Lip link—The man places a kiss on the upper lip of the woman, while the woman lightly sucks the man's lower lip.

Tulips (two lips) kiss—A kiss with one partner's lips totally enveloping the other's lips.

Clasping kiss—A tulip kiss with sucking. The teeth should play no part in this kiss. (Those with facial hair may not find this kiss appealing.)

Palpitating kiss—A kiss where your lower lip moves in a pulsating fashion.

Nip kiss—Blending a kiss with small cautious nibbles. Usually given on the lips, earlobes, neck, or cheeks.

Handle kiss—You each take hold of the other's ears and draw them in close for a kiss. (Popular between adults and children.)

Vacuum kiss—Barely touching your partner's lips with your own, draw in your breath. (This kiss is also given on the cheeks, neck, and other locations.)

Light switch kiss—Kiss the upper lip and then immediately the lower lip of your partner. Also called the switch kiss.

Morse code kiss—Using long and short kisses, spell out messages to your partner in Morse code. (Note: Both need to know Morse code—this is a great way to learn.)

Deep Kisses

Deep kiss—A kiss where both parties have their lips parted, and the tongues explore and caress the inside of the other's mouth.

Mild maraichinage—A toned-down deep kiss where the tongues lightly touch and then withdraw.

French hummer—A deep kiss where one or both of you make humming sounds.

Tongue-tip tango—With both tongues extended outside the mouth, each gently taps the tip of the other tongue.

Tongue combat—The tongues in playful battle with each other during a deep kiss.

Tongue wrestle—With deep kissing, each of you tries to push the other's tongue back into its respective mouth.

Suction kiss—Creating suction during a deep kiss. (Suction is actively given by one partner and passively received by the other.)

Baby bottle kiss—Draw your partner's tongue into your mouth and then lightly suck on it.

The Hoover—Form a tight seal between your lips and your partner's. Both of you then suck inward to create a vacuum inside your mouths. Reverse the suction before trying to separate, and do not hold this kiss for too long because it can become painful.

The close shave—Lightly hold your partner's tongue between your teeth while your partner moves his or her tongue back and forth. Your teeth will gently scrape or shave the tongue. A popular variation is to suck your partner's tongue into your mouth and then release it so your partner can pull it out.

Loop kiss—Pass the tip of your tongue across your partner's upper lip and then along the lower lip. The movement creates a circle or loop and can be done along the inner or outer side of the lips.

French ear—Explore and caress the inside of your partner's ear with your tongue.

Volley kiss—While deep kissing, the two of you alternate blowing into each other's mouths. The recipient's cheeks should expand.

Blast smack—Each blows into the other's mouth during a deep kiss until the pressure becomes too great and forces the lips to break apart.

Wide World of Kisses

Warm-up kisses—Kissing the nose, forehead, or cheek of your partner before kissing the mouth. (Also called the chaste kiss.)

Brush kiss—In a sweeping motion, your lips lightly brush the lips of your partner.

Brow brush kiss—A brush kiss across the eyebrows.

Cheer up kiss—Usually given to a woman to cheer her up. While the woman is looking down at the ground, the man takes her chin in his hand and softly turns her face upward, then kisses her mouth.

Movie star kiss—Beginning at your partner's fingertips start a trail of kisses that eventually concludes with a dramatic kiss upon your partner's lips.

Butterfly kiss—Flutter your eyelashes in place of your lips to kiss your partner. Popular butterfly kiss locations are the cheeks, lips, ears, and eyes. Also called the eyelash kiss.

Electric kiss—On a cool, dry night when the air is overloaded with electricity, the two of you shuffle your feet furiously on a carpet. When you both have a charge, lean over and slowly aim for each other's lips. With your lips about a half-inch apart, move in even slower until a spark jumps between the two of you. Instantly after this happens, kiss one another. You may have to practice this kiss several times in order to master it successfully. The natural reaction is to pull away.

However, the pleasure is the kiss right after the shock. (If done in the dark, you'll see a spark.)

Teasing kiss—Just before the two of you exchange a kiss, draw back and smile at your partner until you can stay away no more. Then slowly move in for the kiss.

Stolen kiss—A stolen kiss is given fleetingly and spontaneously, taking the recipient by surprise. The initiator feigns disbelief of his or her own actions. Both parties must immediately move on after the exchange to eliminate the possibility of any further pursuit.

Backstairs kiss—Similar to the stolen kiss, but more passionate, this is popular at parties or gatherings where guests can pretend to be tipsy or out of control. Most often performed in unusual locations such as behind a door or tree, or on the backstairs. The risk of being discovered in the act is the key element.

Finger kiss—First kiss your index finger. Then lightly touch your index finger to your partner's lips. (Can also be done using your three middle fingers.)

Pendulum kiss—Your lips begin lightly touching one side of your partner's forehead, then brush softly across to the other side where you imprint a kiss. This kiss can also start at a corner of the mouth, lightly moving to the other corner to plant a kiss.

Fingertip kiss—Kiss the tips of your partner's fingers in a fairly quick succession. (Make sure your kisses aren't too wet.)

Profile kiss—Place a series of light kisses along the profile of your partner's face. You may begin at the forehead or the chin. If you start at the forehead, conclude with a pressure kiss on the lips.

Brow kiss—Use light nip kisses on the eyebrows. Make sure not to pull the brow hairs too hard.

Tinguian kiss—Place your lips near your partner's face and suddenly inhale.

Eskimo kiss—Lightly rub your partner's nose with your own from side to side.

Oceanic kiss—Move your nose rapidly across your partner's face from one cheek to the other. Your noses should bump en route.

Kissing Escape Tactics:

- Fake a nose bleed.
- Put a piece of food between your front teeth.
- Stick a plug of chewing tobacco in your mouth.
- Start coughing.
- Blow your nose.
- Filibuster.
- Let your dog kiss you.
- Accidentally set off the burglar alarm.

Dog kiss—Generate short, quick breaths through your nose to imitate a dog sniffing. Then move your nose around the face and/or neck of your partner the same way a dog would.

Nineteenth-century Mongolian kiss—Press your nose to your partner's cheek. Inhale through your nose and smack lips noisily.

Olfactory kiss—Place your nose near or against your partner's face then inhale through it. Also called the smell kiss.

Laplander kiss—Kiss with your lips covering both the mouth and nose of your partner.

Pig kiss—Burrow your nose and mouth into the nape of your partner's neck and snort like a pig.

Kissy-face kiss—Shower your partner's face with light kisses in quick succession.

Rose garden kiss—The woman kisses the man over his entire body, leaving markings of where she's just kissed with tiny lipstick "Xs."

Kiss à l'orange—Each of you places an orange quarter in your mouth, peel side showing, and then kiss.

Traffic light kiss—While stopped in a car at a traffic light, kiss your partner. (When the light changes, the kiss stops.)

Nape kiss—Lightly brush the lips up and down the back of the neck, which is an erogenous zone for many.

Clown kiss—The woman applies heavy lipstick to her lips and then kisses the man all over his face, leaving him with smeared lipstick marks.

The corte—Two pecks followed by two pressured kisses.

Limbo kiss—Beginning just under the chin, the man showers light kisses down the woman's front until she stops him by touching his chin with her hand and pulling his lips up to hers for a kiss. (Named after the game of limbo where the challenge is to see how low you can go.)

Figure-eight kiss—Similar to the limbo kiss. The man kisses downward until the woman guides his head back up and starts kissing downward again. The movement follows the shape of a figure eight.

Backbone kiss—A series of light kisses along the entire backbone, beginning just underneath the neck and traveling downward (stopping at your own discretion).

The window-wiper—Pass the tip of the tongue along your partner's upper lip from left to right and then from right to left. This kiss may also be given inside the mouth. The movement would be the same, but the tongue would instead move along the roof of the mouth.

Tacking kiss—A series of kisses following a path that changes direction after each kiss. Named for the sailing term. Also known as the zigzag kiss.

Miscellaneous Kisses

Good morning kiss—The kiss given in the morning. Most of the time eyes are closed, aim is poor, and breath is bad.

Makeup kiss—The kiss given when you feel sorry about something, or you know you should feel sorry about something.

Boo-boo kiss—A kiss given to those places that have been hurt, cut, scraped, or bruised. Also called the first-aid kiss.

Frog kiss—A kiss given in the hope that when you open your eyes your partner will have transformed into a handsome prince or princess.

Canine kiss—The kiss you get from your adoring dog. It's always wet and always given affectionately.

Chicken kiss—The head darts forward and back in a split second, dispensing a quick peck with no lip.

Forehead kiss—The kiss you get on your forehead from a person you're crazy for, though he or she knows you're too young.

Look-both-ways kiss—A kiss given by people who don't like to be seen kissing so they will swing their head in both directions to see if anyone might be looking.

Sandpaper kiss—A kiss with an unshaven man.

Letter kiss—Kissing a letter and leaving lip prints. Lip prints can be left using lipstick, grape juice, chocolate milk, ink pad—whatever.

Telephone kiss—Simulating a kiss into the telephone receiver for the benefit of the person at the other end.

Training kiss—Any kiss to a mirror or pillow for the purpose of practicing kissing.

Blown kiss—Kiss your hand, then point it toward the kissee and blow. Used when the kissee is not in touching range.

Thrown kiss—Kiss your hands, then wave it in the kissee's direction. Used when the kissee is at a distance.

Hurled kiss—Rotate your upper body clockwise while holding your hand to your mouth. Now, unwind while extending your hand. Made popular on the TV show *The Dating Game*. Used when the kissee is at a very far distance.

Dip kiss—The man holds the woman in the dip dancing position, says something corny like "Kiss me baby," then lays a mushy kiss on her.

Vampire kiss—A hickey on the neck.

This collection of kisses is in no way inclusive. You can create your own or alter one of the above with touch, pressure, sound, passion, tongue, nipping, sucking, brushing, speed, quantity, lip position, or length.

Working from the top on down, these are the most widely enjoyed locations on a person to be kissed: top of the head, forehead, temples, eyelids, eyebrows, tip of the nose, on the ears, earlobes, in the hollow behind the cheeks, above the upper lip and below the tip of the nose, lips, corners of the mouth, chin, back of neck, hollow of the neck, side of the neck, shoulders, shoulder

Rules for Kissing

1. Always hit your target fairly and squarely.
2. Aim for the mouth, but feel free to make use of your hands.
3. Keep it moving. A kiss can last as long as you like.
4. Remember to come up for air. Fainting on a first date is not cool.
5. Boys: Remember this is not a race. It's the breaststroke, not a fast crawl.
6. Girls: Watch the lipstick if you don't want to end up looking like you both had a run-in with a jam tart.
7. Try a bit of nibbling and nuzzling, but no biting—hickeys aren't for the sharp, smart, and sassy.
8. Always keep some gum handy to avoid that "I just ate an anchovy pizza" excuse.

blades, down the backbone, underarm, inside surface of the arm, wrists, inner elbow, palms, fingertips, eyebrows, hollow of the knees, breast bone, arches of the feet, toes.

Final Lip Service

WE HUMAN BEINGS were meant to kiss. We are perfectly configured for the activity. We communicate standing upright, face-to-face, and eye-to-eye. Our lips protrude, our tongues extend, our heads gyrate, and our arms embrace. The only possible addition might have been a tail to wag in delight.

Kissing is a kind of art. It should be constantly refined and never neglected. It is also the most intimate method we have for communicating with our partner. It ripens our emo-

tional and physical understanding of each other and fuels intimacy.

My goal has been to open your eyes and mind to the endless possibilities of kissing. I hope you are now aware of those kissing techniques which achieve maximum results and make you a more proficient kisser. I also hope that along the way you have been enlightened, amused, and eager to find a partner to experiment with.